Gi[...]

Mountains for

My Horses

Give Me Mountains for My Horses

Journeys of a Backcountry Horseman

Tom Reed

Skyhorse Publishing

Skyhorse Publishing may be purchased in bulk at special discounts for sales promotion, corporate gifts, fund-raising, or educational purposes. Special editions can also be created to specifications. For details, contact the Special Sales Department, Skyhorse Publishing, 307 West 36th Street, 11th Floor, New York, NY 10018 or skyhorsebooks@skyhorsepublishing.com.

Skyhorse Publishing® is a registered trademark of Skyhorse Publishing, Inc.®, a Delaware corporation.

Visit our website at www.skyhorsepublishing.com.

10 9 8 7 6 5 4 3 2 1

Library of Congress Cataloging-in-Publication Data is available on file.

Cover design by Tom Lau
Cover photo credit: Thomas Reed

Print ISBN: 978-1-5107-2089-3
Ebook ISBN: 978-1-5107-2090-9

Printed in the United States of America

Contents

—

ONE

The Partnership

—

There is this place. This time. Nothing is behind you and everything ahead. But you don't really think about what is ahead, you only think of now, for this partnership you have entered into is one of the moment, of now. The now has you in a saddle, on a bay horse, heading up a trail of pine and spruce and mountain and stream and meadow.

Behind you, connected to you by only your hand and a lead rope, but carrying everything important to you, is another bay horse, an almost identical match to the one you are riding. You call them nicknames as if they are drinking buddies. Horse in form, but human in heart. You cluck and coo and talk to them as if they give a damn. You think they do. Maybe, just maybe. Right now they are stepping out, heads nodding, heading down the trail, through the stream, and all you have to do is ride. So you ride.

That evening as dusk brings the mosquitoes up out of the willows—the same dusk that put the horseflies to bed—you choose a camp. It is a good place, save for the bugs, with a meadow that lies broad before you and room for the horses out in the deep green and camp back against the lodgepoles, your kitchen down a ways. So you ease off the bay's back and stretch your muscles with that stiff, but good, worked-hard feeling and straighten your back and begin to unload the pack horse. Talking to him. Thanking him. In a while, he has on the hobbles and is out there with his buddies, swishing a long coal-black tail at the mosquitoes and snorting contentedly in the tall grass. You decide it's time to get cracking before dark.

The tent goes up quickly and a meal is eaten down on the gravel bar and the sound of a nighthawk chirping and peeling through the dimming sky, a sound like the tearing of notepaper, and all is well with the world. This is the world. And you haven't thought about anything but this world and you don't even think about not thinking about the other world.

At dawn you rise in the cool and soak in it before the bugs get up. A cup of coffee steams in your palm and it is cool enough for wool and you watch the horses and stand and sip. You turn an ear to the sound of sandhill cranes from somewhere down the meadow. The horses have their heads up at the peculiar sound and you tell them, "Don't worry boys, they don't eat horses" and they go back to their grazing, as if they understand what you just said and maybe, just maybe.

As the day warms and the wool is packed, you work fluidly and quickly. Everything has a routine: the packing, the padding, the hefting, and weighing. It must balance and feel right and go well on those straight good equine backs or it will be off and your day will be long and uncomfortable. There is a lesson here, you think, a lesson of life.

You turn out of camp and saddle the horses and kick their manure around so that it will break down quickly and you look around. Satisfied. The place looks untouched except for a little chewed grass. You swing up and feel those tight muscles again and damn, it feels good to be on a horse headed into wild country.

It goes like this for days, the ride, the squeak of saddle leather. The smell of dust, the taste of it on your tongue. The smell of horse sweat and your own and the feel of soft muzzles nuzzling you after a long day. Gently. Camp after camp. Muscles turning hard with the riding. Eyes sharp for wildlife. And riding, always riding. In camp, meals quickly eaten and your belly full. Of present tense. Carpe diem. And you ride.

One evening, a big sow grizzly and her cub cross a broad meadow far out there, rambling, tough gal, giving you and the horses a wide berth and the binoculars sweating in your hands and your mouth dry.

"Boy, what a beautiful animal."

The next morning, a moose takes her place and walks the same path. You haven't seen another human in days and there's a jet contrail up there reminding you that yes, this is the modern world. You ride.

Another day you cross the river as the Crow and Shoshone and Jim Bridger did long before you. On a horse. Your feet get wet because the river is slow and wide, but deep. A big cutthroat trout as long as your forearm fins off beneath your horse's belly in the clear water and you are glad there's a fly rod cased on the packhorse.

That evening you cast and lose yourself in the rhythm of it, feeling the rod in your hand, casting and drifting and catching another cutthroat, a pure native, whose ancestors swam this same river in the time of the Shoshone and Crow. The horses are out there, deserving a rest day, a layover in your ride and you hear them snorting occasionally and if you listen closely you can hear too that quiet swish of tail. And your heartbeat.

At dawn you rise and saddle and pack and ride up through the burns of '88, where the charred carcasses of lodgepole line your path like mile markers stretching into the horizon as far as you can see. Their trunks are as black as the legs of those fine-legged bays you ride and pack. Dead trees, life at their feet. Fireweed and brush and berries and other flowers by the thousands. Some of the trees have dropped and their bodies are strewn across your path. You cut the few you can and go around those you can't. By mid afternoon, you are in a basin below the big pass that will push you up over the Continental Divide into another basin. When you get there a line of elk, a thin band of only bulls head out before you through old snow, up and over the far peak, making time, walking single file. Up here, up high, away from the bugs that torment their soft and growing antlers, away from everything but blue sky and wildflower-splattered mountain meadow. The next morning you will cross the pass and that is all there is.

The days melt away in the summer heat of the high mountain sun and you catch more fish and see more elk and ride more miles. There are places with names that sing to you, and places without names that hum just as beautifully. You see more moose, two big bulls high up a narrow creek, jogging before your horses high-kneed and pacey gaited and there's a wolf track in the mud and a grizzly scat as big as an elk calf's head.

Two nights before your last one in these high wild mountains you sit with your back against the skin of an old log and you have a mug of hot coffee in your hand and look out across the meadow. There, out there, they move and feed and flick their tails and one has his head up, ears forward looking off into the distance as if he's standing guard over the rest.

And while you are looking at them, belly full, hands warm, nestled in there in the pine needles and columbines you realize: what an amazing thing to have an animal carry your hide up and over and through and beyond. This is connection, the element that is everything. Partnership. A bond between man and animal that has lasted for thousands of years and only in the last one hundred has been forgotten by most. This is the animal that has carried your people to war and peace and beyond and then home and here is the connection and you think how damn lucky you are to have found it. It is a good, rich life, this life of yours. It is here before you and this partnership brings the balance to your being, the straightening of things so you can walk right and do well.

I've known all my life there was something special about horses. There are old family photos of me aboard a dude horse, a trusty, tired old fellow that had probably carried thousands of little boys up easy mountain trails. I was four and my feet didn't even come close to touching the stirrups. I had both hands on the saddle horn, as if I was trying to tear the thing right off. In the photo, I'm grinning. If I close my eyes and concentrate, I can almost feel myself there, almost grasp that memory, smell the dusted manure drifting in the summer corral, feel that animal beneath me, hear it snort and paw impatiently. Perhaps these thoughts live because those times were rare and unique, and thus memorable. But perhaps these fragments transcend time because I knew even then, even at four, that I belonged on horseback, riding into the mountains, going somewhere, seeing new things, new country.

It wasn't until I was an adult that I actually owned a horse of my own, and felt that connection of souls that has carried many human-horse relationships throughout time. When I could finally afford a horse and find a place for pasture, I purchased a truck and a trailer and all the gear that goes along with the ownership of such an animal.

That first time, that first horse of my own took me there. One word describes the experience: transformed. Gave me another way of looking at the world. I've spent my whole life in the mountains and desert, outside where I can breathe. But I never really saw the country. Moving down a trail on an animal you care for, looking ahead, seeing elk and deer, traveling timber and meadow, fording big streams swollen with snowmelt. That's seeing it.

A friend once asked me if it was expensive to own a horse and I thought about the price of hay, and of pasture, of worming, vaccinations, shoes. Those expenses were the easy ones. I told him about the other costs. If you own horses, you want to take them somewhere. So, you'll need a trailer, and you'll need a truck and you'll need a saddle and other gear. These are the true costs of owning a horse. And, if you would like to live near your horses, to be able to crack open the kitchen window on a warm spring morning and say something intelligent or otherwise to your trusty steed, you'll need a piece of horse pasture all your own. Those are expenses, but the emotional dividends wash them all away.

There will be a special horse, a horse that takes the tough trails, that gets you home. Perhaps there will be more than one. This partnership of man and horse is nothing new. Alexander the Great rode a fine black stallion named Bucephalus. General Robert E. Lee led the Confederate Army from the back of an iron-gray Saddlebred named Traveller. He bought Traveller in 1861 in the mountains of Virginia and rode him throughout the war to that final day at Appomattox Court House. Another Civil War horse was Rienzi, a black Morgan ridden by Union General Philip Sheridan during the Union victory at Cedar Creek, Virginia. His alleged ride of seventy-five miles in a day aboard Rienzi was immortalized in the poem "Sheridan's Ride" and the ride inspired the retreating Union soldiers to rally and turn defeat into victory.

But it was in the open West, the big empty, that the partnership of man and horse gained its full glory. General George Custer chased down bison aboard his horses Vic and Dandy. Buffalo Bill Cody had Charlie, purchased in 1872 when he scouted for the Army. Charlie went on to star in his Wild West show. Cody also owned Brigham, Powder Face, Buckskin Joe, and Tall Bull, all horses that propelled him into fame. Then there were the horses of Hollywood—William S. Hart's Fritz, Tom Mix astride Tony, Gene Autry and Champion, Roy Rogers and Trigger. Partners. The famous naturalist writer Aldo Leopold, used horses to define wilderness: "By 'wilderness' I mean a continuous stretch of country preserved in its natural state, open to lawful hunting and fishing, big enough to absorb a two weeks' pack trip . . ." he wrote in 1921. His horse was a gray gelding he called Polly.

For me, I want a horse that will get down the trail, a stepping-out, go-to-town type of animal that enjoys going somewhere and seeing what's over the next ridge. There are horses and there are mountain horses. Mine have all been mountain horses. Taken alone, they move your soul. Taken together, they move your life.

TWO

A Man Named Jim and a Horse Named Todd

—

When I was young, I dreamed of horses.

Walls of reality bind the dreams of men, but the dreams of boys have no boundaries. Boys dream big. Mine happened to be horses. I do not know where this dream was born, but it grew on the land, a land that itself seemed to have little edge other than forests and a highway that went to the city in one direction and to the mountains in the other. The world was bound by ponderosa pine and bunch grass. Beyond the trees were mountains and big open country.

Our home sat in the foothills west of Denver and west of Denver in the 1960s was pretty far out there. Denver itself was a small city then, still defining itself, separated from the other towns along Colorado's Front Range by miles of open road and farmland. The foothills then were little different from the 1800s when Denver was a supply town for the gold camps of the Rockies.

South of our home rose a mountain of pine called Genesee. To the north lay Clear Creek Canyon, wild, full of elk and deer and bears. My home was beyond the fence line. Open space. Beyond the fence was a small herd of bison. They were shaggy and massive and they smelled wild. The herd was owned and cared for by Denver Mountain Parks, held in a pasture of several hundred acres for the tourists to enjoy. An eight-foot fence is really nothing for a boy. The bison herd was cautiously skirted—I was bold, but not stupid. Beyond that more wild country and a whole world.

It was a boy's playground and if you wanted to spend a day getting lost in chasing things like bugs and butterflies and bigger quarry like squirrels and hapless jays, you could. Houses were few, roads fewer and there were no rules. There was no separation of boy and land, boy and nature. It was as if I were part of it and it a part of me.

The bison, perhaps, kept the dream of horses alive, that and my father's admiration of the artist Charlie Russell. I saw these bison on a Russell canvas, on a wide-open prairie where their numbers were uncountable. I saw myself in these visions, on a horse, rifle in one hand, reins in the other, caught up in the frontier. Those fenced bison behind my house were hardly the same as their wild ancestors, but they were enough.

It was a big landscape, beckoning. Juniper and aspens and ponderosa and pasque flowers and spring beauties growing in the wake of snowmelt. Requiring a horse and a horseman. I guess I figured it might be handy to be carried across that landscape and that four legs are always better than two.

My maternal grandmother fed this dream as well. She lived with us when I was a boy, and helped get me down the path to a lifetime spent outdoors. She read stories to me in a soft, kind voice—Will James, Laura Ingalls Wilder, Ralph Moody, who wrote a series of books about ranches and horses in Colorado—but she also had a dream of owning her own land and that dream was realized before I was out of grade school. Perhaps more than anything, the land that she purchased in the late sixties in south-central Colorado's Fremont County had an impression on me and, coupled with growing up with wild country at my toes, horses were galloping in my head. As a child, she had a burro named Hot Biscuit and she showed me faded black- and-white photos of the white burro with a little girl in a dress astride. I made no distinction between donkey and horse.

Her house lay at the base of a big mountain, where sixty years earlier a famous grizzly bear had been gunned down after raising hell with the area's cattle and sheep. She had about four hundred acres of deeded ground, mostly aspen, but also some ponderosa and limber pine, blue and Engelmann spruce, and Douglas fir.

To the east rose Pikes Peak, to the north the aptly named timbered flank of Black Mountain, and far to the south was the canyon of the Arkansas. In that chunk of country where I spent my summers, I found plenty to dream about and a library full of books to carry me there. My grandmother leased the grazing rights to a wind-chiseled old man. He'd show up on a stout sorrel horse and I remember standing on the porch talking to him as he sat the horse with a comfort and ease that made him look just like those cowboys in Charlie Russell's paintings. I had to have a horse.

Back home and back in school, I tried to convince Dad that we had room. The family across the road owned horses, two or three, kept in a small corral. We could build something like that too. The neighbor girls down the road owned an old sway-backed gray mare, and across the valley, another family with a collection of pigs and chickens and assorted barnyard friends had a foul-tempered Shetland pony. It bit and bucked and left me with the impression that all ponies are irritable, like a short man with a Napoleonic complex. Not surprisingly, the neighbors were open to the possibility of selling that fine steed and I ran the idea past Dad. It wasn't a black stallion, but, like the bison herd and their pasture, it would do. It tried to roll every time you hopped onto its bony hide, but that didn't matter. It was a horse to me as much as the bison were wild.

My father somehow held this idea at bay long enough for me to become distracted, as boys are, by other things like hunting and fishing and football. I never did get that horse I wanted as a boy and eventually, the dream faded and flickered, barely alive. It would be fed occasionally by a glimpse of a horse in a pasture somewhere, or a horse and rider on some far ridge.

Our neighbor went on elaborate pack trips and came back telling of mountains and horses, good food and laughter, as if all four elements fit together like pieces of a puzzle. I listened to those stories and I thought of horses from time to time and I kept reading. And yet, the reality of actually owning a horse eluded me. When I left Colorado for college in Arizona, that dream had all but faded to black.

By the time I graduated from the university, my sole experiences with horses were getting bit by that Shetland, falling off the neighbor girls' old horse when the three of us were riding bareback, and taking the occasional drunken gallop on a listless dude horse during some college fraternity event. The mountains and horses and the trails I would ride were years away.

Some years after graduation I found myself in charge of a newspaper, a position that I greeted with both surprise and an edge of cockiness that startles me still. Surprise, because I knew nothing about the newspaper business and cockiness because I thought I did.

The newspaper was owned by a Texan who had a summer home in Colorado, an oil man who cared little if the paper made money, and paid even less attention to the editorial pages or the content of the news. There is no truer platform for the First Amendment than that. With fervor, I attacked, loving the power of my words to incite a blizzard of letters to the editor, a change in government policy, a red-faced visit from the college president. It was a heady feeling for a young man in his mid-twenties.

The town where I lived was in the heart of southwestern Colorado, surrounded on all sides by mountains and wildness. It spoke to me and I thought about those flung-back places in the wilderness where you could hunt elk and fly fish for wild trout. I wrote a few editorials defending wild country and places to hunt and fish.

Later that year, the surrounding National Forest released a plan to log hundreds of acres of aspen to feed a waferboard plant in a nearby town. Up to that point aspen cut off of private land kept the mill going, but that supply was slowly dwindling and the lumber conglomerate that owned the plant was pushing for a cut on public land. Their appetite was huge and it was for trees on land that belonged to everybody. Therein lay the problem. Like most rural western communities, the country was the big attraction, and the reason we all lived there on thin wages. Most people in a small western town will tell you they'd rather see elk on a high ridge than drive a new car every year.

The proposed logging was to be immense, pushing up against wilderness areas, punching roads into aspen groves that were elk calving grounds. For a person who liked to hunt and fish and didn't mind a good walk in the woods, it was a disaster. And I said as much.

Two days later, the phone rang. The voice had depth, a resonance and character to it like distant thunder rolling across a sagebrush sea. He introduced himself.

"I like the way you editorialize. Do you have a day this week? I want to take you on a ride."

It was June, a month of summer and winter rolled together, squeezed between July and the latest big freeze in tall country.

I looked at my calendar.

"Well, my schedule is pretty open for the latter part of the week."

"Good, I'll have a horse for you."

It is raining when we meet on Friday morning, the sky close, heavy with moisture. Gray-blue. His name is Jim and he's tall and wears a mustache and a Stetson. I am at a table in the town's café, one cup of coffee down already. He stands between the twin glass doors and pulls his hat off, shaking it once, twice, as one would shake the paint out of a brush, the moisture spraying the inner glass door. I have never met him, but the voice fits the man. I extend a hand.

We each order biscuits and gravy and work our way through weak coffee and get-acquainted talk. Where'd you grow up? You like to hunt birds? Fishing? How long you been married? Outside, the rain gets heavier, the streets filling and the rushing wet sound of each passing car coming through the café's windows. Streaks of snow mix with the rain, letting us know that winter is not too distant and could, in fact, come again.

Jim hasn't yet told me where we are going, but I trust that at minimum, there's a story. There has to be a story. I can't burn a weekday without getting something done, something accomplished. The newspaper's staff is small, and it's a strain to fill those pages.

"Much of an elk hunter?"

"I love to hunt. I can't get enough of it." I'm wondering, in fact, how I am going to fit a full-time job into my hunting this fall. "I'll bet you know all the places?"

He smiles. "Oh, there's a lot of them around this country."

No hunter gives away his best spot to someone he met over breakfast. "Tell me what you know about horses."

"That's a short story. I've always wanted to have horses. That's about all I can tell you."

"Well, you'll get along with old Mike okay. He's pretty gentle. We're going up on West Antelope. Amazing country. You'll like it."

West Antelope is a long, thin ridge that rises above a state-owned wildlife area and extends back into the high country. At its base, sage and wild blue flag grow in the moist soil. The ridge rises and the sage gives way to pockets of aspen and then the pockets become groves and the groves become a huge forest of aspen, some with trunks larger than a man's hug. At the top of it, up against the West Elk Wilderness and even higher country, the aspen surrender to Engelmann spruce and lush meadows, then timberline and the highest country.

He tells me this and he talks of the land as if it were a child, a living being, not soil and wood and wildlife. He runs a bookstore now, he tells me, and the authors on his shelves specialize in writing about wild places and wild things. Most of the authors are long dead, but their words live on. But before the store, he worked for the state's fish and game department, and this was his district. For years he fought a transfer to Denver since he disagreed with his supervisors. The bureaucrats in the capital city would regularly come down on the opposite side of wildlife, while Jim held pure. He held them off long enough, and he held off others who wanted to punch roads into the backcountry, who wanted to cut trees without regard to elk. At the end, though, he tired of it all and when there came a chance for an early retirement, he jumped.

The last battleground was West Antelope. Against the wilderness area, where a jeep road ran between the pale trunks of aspen, the Forest Service proposed a timber cut. This was hunting country and the road up was rough enough to keep the camps scattered and the hunting good. It was also a place of birth, where the elk cows each spring find hidden corners in the thick aspen each spring, where the cycle would start all over again. The aspen forests were lush and clogged with fern and wildflower. A spotted new elk calf curled in a tight ball disappeared in such a jungle. A new road in such a country? Disaster for hunters and elk calves alike.

The road to the cut would be suitable for a sedan, and the clear cuts would be wide. It wasn't the cut, he said. Logging was one thing. But not here, not in one of the most important elk calving grounds of the valley, not against a wilderness area boundary. Aspen could be cut somewhere, but this was not the place. Worse, the logging road would run up through that state wildlife area, an area purchased and preserved for wintering elk and deer. The road is to be shut down in winter, but it is the principle of the thing, and while breakfast is going down, I understand that this is a man of principle, and without it, there can be nothing else. He was born in this country, and he wants to see it stay as it is, a good place to live, a place to ride a good mountain horse, a place with elk on a wind-scoured ridge. And that is principle enough for any two men.

We step out into the rain and I realize that I'm completely unprepared. I've forgotten any kind of hat, but Jim has an extra slicker tied behind the saddle that I'm going to ride. As we head west of town in his pickup, our talk swings between hunting, fishing, books, the land. His voice is one of those that you could listen to for hours, for it has a smoothness to it.

Just west of town, Jim gears the truck down and turns north, off the pavement, heading toward the wildlife area. The truck fishtails a bit in the mud and the two-horse trailer sloshes back and forth. Mud splatters the windshield, the wheel-wells, the trailer behind us, and I can feel the horses rocking back there, swaying off-balance, then the truck is right again. Jim gears down even more and grinds along the road in the glop. A few years ago, this place was a ranch, but now the hay in the meadows is harvested, stored for a tough winter when the elk gather on ridges and die by the hundreds. This place will winter several thousand head, even in the toughest Colorado winter. It sits back at the end of a valley against a gray flank of sage. The meadows are greening with the coming spring. Even on this dull day, the green is brilliant, alive. Summer is coming, but not without a little hard work.

Mike the horse is a tall gray, stout and unremarkable in looks except for his size. Jim's horse is also fairly unremarkable, at least to my untrained eye. His name is Todd and he's the kind of bay that is so brown that most people just call the color brown. He has a star and he's about fifteen hands high. Jim tells me this, for I do not know how to measure horses.

The horses scramble backward out of the two-horse trailer and I watch my feet as hooves pivot over the wet ground. Jim hands me Mike's lead rope. "Tie him up over there, left side."

I work on a square knot.

"Here, let me show you a better knot."

His strong hands undo my work, and then retie a loop that can be pulled on one end and loosened from the trailer. A slipknot.

"This way, if the horse pulls back, the knot isn't so tight you can't get it undone. Plus, you can get to the horse quick and get him loose if he gets into trouble."

It is a lesson in horsemanship. Brushing, blanketing, saddling, bridling. I take mental notes and watch how the man moves around his horses, always aware of where his feet are, and what the horses are doing. He walks behind them and he talks to them in that voice of his, and he puts his hands on them. On their necks, their rumps, their backs, their noses. Mike is gentle enough and quiet. He waits nose-down by the trailer, almost dozing in the cold rain. The other one is different and I'm beginning to see this already. There is a character to him. Todd has his head up, ears forward, and is looking in every direction. He even whinnies occasionally, loud enough and close enough to my ears to make me wince. He paws the ground and he dances on the lead rope tied to the trailer and he smears the mud at his hooves into a mess. He's the kind of horse that makes you move quickly about him, at least if you are a rookie in such things. Jim, though, doesn't seem to notice and when he's near the bay horse, his hand is on him and his voice is in the air.

"Todd still thinks he's a stud. He's proud cut."

I don't ask what that means, but I have a feeling that Jim wouldn't laugh if I did. He'd just tell me.

I watch as Jim backs Todd away from the trailer, now bridled and saddled. Ready. The horse is now quieter, standing still so the man can climb on, as if he knows that he's going nowhere without the man on his back. And he does want to go. Jim stands by the horse's head, turns a stirrup, left foot up and in, and in one smooth motion, he's up there. The horse spins on its hind end and steps out three steps, nose forward, neck arched.

I try the same thing with Mike, turning the stirrup, standing up by the head. It's a long way off the ground for my left leg, and I can feel my hamstring tightening. I struggle with the reins in the same hand as the saddle horn and I try to make sense of it all, a sensation that is uncoordinated and embarrassing all at the same time. Okay, now swing up.

I get about four inches off the ground and the whole works— saddle, pad, saddlebags—turns to the side. It's about all I can do to not fall flat on my butt in the mud.

"Damn."

"Oh, Mike's so round it's kind of hard to get on him." Chuckling. Not an out-and-out laugh, but a chuckle. I can feel my face reddening.

"Well, I'll try that again."

I work my foot into the stirrup again and try to swing up. The saddle turns again. Jim is looking down at me from Todd and there's a grin on his face. At least he isn't slapping his knee and hooting with laughter, but it probably wouldn't matter. It is still not the way to start out my cowboy career. I try again and this time, claw my way up. Not the fluid motion of my new friend, but enough. I'm on. It feels good to be aboard if only to hear the laughter subside.

We ride up through the sage in the early morning drizzle. Ahead of us run Jim's two dogs, English setters named Ned and Jed. Jed is a pup and he moves through the brush with the awkwardness of growing legs and big feet, but I can see a grace in him as well, an underlying, barely hidden style that will become a promising bird dog. Ned is that kind of dog, speckled black and white, fluid in motion and range. They work the sage well together, dancing back and forth, leaping over brush, then pointing meadowlarks, sage sparrows, the occasional sage grouse. The pup even honors the old dog, pointing at the older dog's point, backing his play.

It is wet riding, but the rain has slacked. The old jeep road is soft and slick, and Mike slides occasionally. There's a tangy sweetness in the air that washes across the land and blends with the earthy smell of mud. An optimistic lark gives voice from a stand of sage and I see him, yellow breast shining even on this dull day in this olive-gray ocean of sage.

I get used to the saddle, its sounds, its feel. I love how it creaks beneath my weight and I can feel the ride and the movement of the horse beneath. I take a tip or two from Jim, and ride as he rides. Heels down, reins in one hand, sitting on his back pockets. Talking as if he wasn't on a horse at all, but on a chair in his own living room. He looks natural, straight, right. I straighten my spine, sit on my hip pockets, imitate the man.

We enter the first knot of aspen after a long ride up the bench, climbing several hundred, perhaps even a thousand feet above the valley floor. The sky is still close and dim, and we can't see the basin itself, but just over the ridge is the town we both call home and we can feel it out there, lying on the valley bottom.

The first grove smells of damp leaves and growing buds. The aspen have leafed out, but the leaves are small, only the size of dimes. It is a reminder of the earliness of the season. We ride beneath and deeply breathe of moist soil and leaves. The trunks of the aspen are scarred by the teeth of elk and deer, rubbed by cattle. Human signs too—initials, brands. On the bark of one particularly large tree, the shapely, beautifully-carved form of a naked woman. Dated 1945. The biggest of the trees is perhaps two and a half feet in diameter, big for a short-lived aspen, stout and still strong. The biggest trees have limbs as thick as a man's thigh.

"This is where the cut will start. In this grove. They plan on working in patches all the way up to the high country, and into the spruce. They'll do selective cutting up there, but this is clear cutting down in the aspen. Aspen bounce back pretty quick after being disturbed. But that isn't the point. That darned road is the point. It's going to ruin this country. This is elk country. Should stay that way."

An hour later, Ned and Jed jump a small band of cow elk and six of them move off in the green timber, hides of vanilla and rust flashing through the trees, the snap of a branch, another, and then another, marking their passing. Todd whinnies at them, a bellow that rings through the trees and echoes back on us. Jim whistles the dogs in and they pant at heel behind Todd for a while until the elk have moved well off and then there's a brisk "okay" from their boss and they are off again, plowing headlong into the wetness.

Ever since we entered the aspen, things have changed. Out in the sage, though the sky was close, there was a bigness to the land, an openness that matched a life horseback. In the grove, everything is lush and heavy and verdant. Huge ferns cover the ground between the white trunks of the trees, and there is life everywhere. The sage was scattered, but here everything is thick.

The rain starts again, and I'm wishing I had thought to bring a hat. Jim offers his hat cover, a glorified plastic bag that can fit over a Stetson. But the incident with the horse mounting was bad enough without riding through the timber with a bag over one's head. I politely pass. He chuckles. "Well, suit yourself. Hope you don't catch a cold."

Noon finds us at an old cabin high on the ridge. Or at least, it feels like it's on the ridge. The sky hugs us, down around our ears with rain. It feels as if we are breathing in water. There is no view. The cabin could be on the side of a hill, or it could be in a valley. I have no idea. Jim knows right where he is and reins up in front of the cabin and gets off. My dismount goes a lot smoother than the mount and I work on the new knot I have learned and get it right the second time.

Jim is gracious. "Most people have to learn that knot a couple of times. Good job."

The aspens have given way to the spruce now, and Jim says we are getting near the wilderness boundary. We find a big spruce with limbs that stretch out like a picnic awning. We stoop and are under, sheltered by canopy. Beneath, on a carpet of needles, it's surprisingly dry, dry enough to unbutton my slicker and shake some of the wetness out of my hair. Ned and Jed burrow under there too, and each take a side of their master as he leans back cross-legged against the trunk of the big tree. They are soaked, panting, happy, smelling the way only wet dogs can smell. He shares his lunch with me. Elk jerky, two pickles, a candy bar. Outside, beyond those outstretched limbs of the big spruce, Mike stands lazy footed, three-legged in the rain. He has his head down, but Todd's is up, ears perked forward. He paws the wet grass beneath the fence rail where he is tied and snorts, jigging on his lead rope a bit. He doesn't look happy. Then he cuts loose with a whinny.

"Todd. Relax."

I ask Jim how far we are from the wilderness boundary.

"I'd say about two miles, we'll be looking over right into West Beaver Creek, right into the heart of the West Elks. Good country."

"How far have we come?"

"Oh, I'd guess about six miles."

Todd whinnies again.

I've been watching him as we ride, this little brown horse with a big star and white hind socks. In the hours of mud and rain, even a novice can get to know a horse. This one has been walking out smooth and clean all day, bursting into voice every now and then to be greeted by Jim's soft reprimand. Jim's left arm has been cocked back against the reins. As far as I can tell, he hasn't put a heel to the horse's side. Not once. I've been prodding Mike all day, poking at his side as rookie riders do, trying to get him to keep up with Todd. Although Todd is much smaller, I get the feeling that he could walk the horseshoes right off of Mike.

I ask Jim.

"Oh, Todd can walk. He's the fastest walking horse in the county."

We sit back like this for a while, smelling the sap of the spruce, dry enough on our pad of needles, listening to the rain, watching Todd.

He had been part of a load of horses brought from Missouri to Colorado, a youngster with straight legs and a good eye. A charged young colt, with electricity virtually running through his veins. The colt and his trailer companions came west as the property of the United States Forest Service, which had been buying a particular breed of horses, Missouri Fox Trotters, for some time. These gaited horses could cover ground quickly, were a pleasure to ride, and were, for the most part, calm and gentle for beginning rangers.

Todd had been the exception. He was assigned to the ranger in Creede, a man who knew a bit about horses, but not enough. The colt, though ready to ride, was not a beginner's horse and he was just enough to scare the ranger into asking for another horse. Todd suddenly found himself on the market after only a year in Colorado.

Meanwhile, Jim had been riding the high country on his ranch-bred horses and at times, he found himself in the saddle alongside those Forest Service types and their fast-moving fox trotters.

"I was taking a beating," he says, "physically and emotionally. Those horses at a walk moved better than my old horse at a trot."

Jim made a few phone calls to the Forest Service horse buyer and heard about Todd.

"I showed up at the trader's place with my saddle and horse trailer and in this corral was this lean bay walking a ditch around the inside of the corral fence." He makes a circle with his hand, illustrating the path of the anxious horse inside a corral.

He caught the young bay and threw a saddle on his back. "He had fire. I can still remember getting on him. It was evident that I was astride a bundle of high test energy."

The horse trader opened the gate and down the road Jim went on Todd. "When I got him pulled in from a lope, he showed me his stuff. I was suddenly feeling the smoothest and fastest ground-covering gait I had ever felt."

The sale had been made.

That night, Jim brought the young gelding back to his hometown and left him at a friend's ranch where there was a collection of six-foot-high corrals. There were horses in the neighboring corrals, but in the dark Jim didn't think much about it. It had been a long day and he had a new horse. He was tired.

The next morning when he got to the headquarters he said, "No Todd. The pen where I'd left him was empty, but there was a lot of activity two pens west. The owner of a quarter horse mare was trying valiantly to keep Todd and his very willing mare apart. He was mad as hell and telling me all about this unplanned mating with my gelding. I told him he was a gelding, but he wasn't buying it."

Jim spent the morning repairing some broken corral rails, then took Todd back home and got with the construction of a corral that stood eight feet tall.

Jim offers me another piece of elk jerky. The rain has slacked off somewhat and we could be going, but this story of the horse keeps me anchored against the bark of the big spruce. He is fluid, with a descriptive vocabulary that speaks of books and history. He can tell a tale.

"Well, that next few weeks, I'll bet I rode hundreds of miles in the high country."

Todd walked the legs right out from under all the other horses, including horses being ridden by Forest Service rangers. "Only the very best of them could keep up with him. He was just that fast and that smooth. I was really thinking I had gotten the deal of a lifetime, and a lot of the forest types thought that too.

They couldn't understand why Todd had gotten a dishonorable discharge. Then I went on a pack trip."

It all came together on that trip. Todd wasn't technically a stallion with all of the equipment, but his brain told him he was. During that pack trip, with several mares in the herd, Todd made a fool out of himself.

During the day, Todd was snorty and walked bow-necked among the mares. Jim often found himself riding well ahead of the group in order to control his new horse. At night, Jim kept the amorous horse tied close and hobbled. He laid out his sleeping bag nearby, but one night, while the rest of the camp slept, Jim awoke, glancing over in the thin moonlight to where Todd was tied. "No Todd."

There was a commotion from the meadow where the mares were grazing. Todd had somehow rubbed out of his halter and was out with the other horses attempting to mount a willing mare while wearing hobbles. Jim madly dashed for his boots.

"I did some quick action, but it wasn't too well planned," he laughs. "I ran into the midst of the horse herd with only boots and shorts, with no rope. Suddenly, I was in the middle of an excited bunch of horses with both arms around Todd's neck, wondering what in the heck I was going to do next. The whole camp was still asleep and pride kept me from calling for help."

Todd finally calmed down. "He let me short-step him with hobbles still on over to where I spotted a saddle and bridle lying on the ground."

The randy would-be stallion found himself tied up again, and Jim turned in. No one in the camp had stirred.

The man talks like this for a while, the stories of his favorite horse rolling off of his tongue. It is as if man and horse cannot be separated. They are one thing, one being.

I ask him why he puts up with a horse like that, one that can lose its head in a moment.

"I'll let you ride him someday."

We ride for another hour through a thick stand of spruce and then everything opens up before us. The forest ends and ahead and above is a long thin ridge. As if to welcome us, the sky lifts a bit and we can see far down below, a long thin valley. Far off in a high basin, a thin waterfall threads down through a boulder field, feeding the creek that feeds the stream that carved the valley. It is quiet except for a slight push of wind from the west that whistles past our ears. The snow is still thick up high against the mountain, brilliant white even when lit by a gray day. At our horses' hooves is a carpet of marsh marigolds in the meltwater and for a moment, the sun comes out, casting thin rays over the land before us, splashing gold on the high white peaks, on the ridge above. In one of those beams, well up the ridge at timberline, I see a small herd of elk, no more than a dozen head of cows and calves, orange in the light of it all. We sit our horses for a while and look off into the wildness of it.

We do not speak. There are no words to say. Even Todd is quiet.

THREE

Equine Dreams

—

The first sign that we may be in trouble comes fifty miles south of Cheyenne. A clunk from somewhere below us, near the transmission. We glance at each other and simultaneously ask "Did you hear that?", hoping, perhaps, that the sound is a product of individual imagination. Paranoia. But we both heard it. Southbound traffic whirls around us, heading to Denver. We push on. It is just the one sound, brief enough to fade and be called into question as more highway slips by. In another fifty miles we will have forgotten.

It is early September and the green is fading out of the land. Rows of cut corn standing in huge fields flank both sides of the highway. Other fields grow row after row of new homes, planted in linear symmetry and genetic sameness, stretching toward the horizon. We haven't seen truly open country since the Wyoming border. There is no discernable line demarking the boundaries of the cities of Colorado's Front Range. They blend together. Homogenized. Even the automobiles zipping around us are generic, shiny, new. Our old truck sticks out.

The old red Ford is about done in. The truck has AM radio and the wind whistles through the wing windows, drowning out most of the country music. Conversation, when we have it, is quick and stunted, the kind of talk that covers the bases of communication and not much else. Even outside of noisy old pickup trucks, our conversations are like this, sparse, pragmatic. Talk has been like that for some time now. There is no ceremony, just enough effort to function, like a bachelor eats his dinner standing without fanfare at the kitchen sink. Shoveling. Fuel for the machinery and that is all.

The truck is more than twenty years old and salt used on winter roads has eaten through its skin. Through one corner of the floorboards, I can see the blur of pavement. A battalion of dead flies sprinkles the dashboard. The cab has that old-truck smell, axle grease and dust, and miles of asphalt and dirt road traveled. It is a good odor that reminds me of my grandmother's ranch in southern Colorado, of her old truck and dusty roads and red-winged blackbirds chirping their song from the hay meadow.

The Ford has no frills, no power-anything, but it pulls a load and that will do. Behind us is a borrowed two-horse trailer.

We have enough money between us to buy gas to last until western Colorado, and back to Wyoming. Then we'll be out. The rest will be spent on the horses we are going to pick up and two months' pasture. We are about to embody "horse poor" and because it is my dream and not hers, there is tension in the cab, enough that you can almost hear it over the radio static and wing-window music.

I had wanted them. She went along, thinking I was a bit insane to spend money on horses when we should be thinking about buying a home. But I want the horses. I can be bullheaded that way, set up, no turning back.

We hope to make the in-laws' home in Grand Junction before midnight and as the highway climbs up out of the plains into the mountains, the old truck makes no more ominous sounds. It is dark by the time we crest the foothills and put Denver behind us.

Paul, my horse-trading friend, had called two weeks ago. "I found you two some pretty good horses. A palomino four-year-old and a paint that is eight. I think they'll work for you."

The dream had depth and length, a dream that had become an obsession. I had done enough mountain riding to recognize that I did not need something that I could rope off of, or cut cows with. I wanted a horse like my friend Jim's, a horse that could cover ground and could pack an elk. The elk and deer I shot, I backpacked out of the mountains and when I looked at maps in the long winter, I dreamed of getting farther back in, much deeper in the wilderness than I would travel on foot. An animal that could carry both meat and me would be ideal. I wanted a horse. Always had.

I looked at a nondescript buckskin mare, but I did not know the first thing about buying a horse. So I was tentative and someone else came along and bought the mare before I could make up my mind. Jim recommended Paul, a man who annually brought a certain kind of horse back from Missouri: a fox-trotting horse. Jim's horses were fox trotters too, horses that moved easily and quickly, that did not need constant riding to keep their heads in shape. I wanted one of those and so I called Paul and asked him about horses and described my riding ability—limited—and my wife's—more limited.

When Paul made his annual trek to southern Missouri, he kept us in mind and he found two horses that he thought would do. Now, a borrowed horse trailer, a coworker with some horse pasture and an old Ford and we would have our horses. Just one of the horses cost more than twice as much as the truck.

In the rearview, the lights of Denver twinkle like broken glass caught in headlights, shine on the side of a highway and we climb up out of the flat, up a long canyon where the interstate snakes through the ponderosas. This is my country, where I grew up dreaming of horses and mountains. We crest the foothills and in the darkness, we cannot see the wide range of mountains that looms over the land, the Continental Divide. I know the mountains are there, out in the distant blackness.

We lose the drive shaft just as we crest the ridge. There is a tremendous clanging from beneath and a stream of sparks lights up the night, splashing up against the horse trailer. I wrestle the pickup to the side of the interstate and crawl beneath the truck on the cold pavement.

In anticipation of pulling a horse trailer with an old pickup, I had the clutch replaced. Our neighbor was a nice man who was starting his own mechanic business and I figured I would give him some of ours. The flashlight reveals the depth of my mistake. He forgot to tighten the bolts on the U-joint. Working on the cold pavement, I pull the drive shaft down and throw it into the bed of the pickup. The old truck is four-wheel drive and so I lock in the hubs and crawl it to the next exit. Not one of the one hundred or so cars that passes us stops to offer help. This is not Wyoming by a long shot. The house where I grew up is fortunately only a few miles away and my parents get an unexpected midnight visit. The old Ford ticks as it cools in the driveway and I have a beer to calm my nerves before turning in.

The next morning, my brother and I crawl under the old Ford with a new U-joint, and by noon, we are on our way west toward the horses.

U

Sometimes when I dream of horses, I wake in the middle of the night and think of that first horse and of that morning in Delta, Colorado, when I saw him for the first time. The dream one carries and builds in the mind is never a perfect match for what becomes the reality, but this one comes close. The horse seemed to have a glow all his own, and he paced in the corral beneath the big cottonwoods and whinnied across the desert to the east, back toward home in Missouri.

I wonder how he felt, how the hot dry air coming off the badlands smelled, how everything was strange and fresh and new. He had a fire and I sat there on the corral poles, feeling the rough surface on my palms. I watched my horse pace and stop and whinny and then walk some more. My horse. My horse. I'd been waiting a long time to say those words. I threw a saddle on his back, cinched him, and rode him in the corral and then down the road. Later, we took both of the horses out on the desert and rode them on powdered clay and felt the sun on our forearms and shoulders and laughed at the riding and the feel of it.

Back home in Wyoming, the horse and I tussled. With the borrowed horse trailer returned to its owner, I rode out of the pasture where I kept him, up onto a section of rolling prairie that was owned by the state and rented by a sheepman. The young horse spooked at the sheep and he spooked at glittering objects in the borrow ditch, and he spooked at nothing at all. I rode as best I could, which wasn't very well, and I hung on. Later, we hired a would-be cowboy to give us riding lessons and words of caution came back to me, words that Paul had spoken: "You'll run across a few cowboys who think they know it all, but there aren't many horsemen out there. When you find one of those, listen to him. Don't listen to the cowboys."

The lessons only lasted a few days. The man fancied himself a farrier as well as a horse trainer, so we paid him to shoe the horses. When my young horse leaned on him, the man punched the gelding in the gut with the heel of the rasp. It was a move that was full of anger and quick, an action that carried far less punch than what horses deal out to each other in the herd, but he did it to my horse and that was enough. He loaded his tools and did not come back.

We were back to riding on our own, sometimes circling the pasture, sometimes braving the borrow pit and the sheep herd. Always learning. The yellow horse spun in circles and he snorted at strange things. Once, on a flat slick with snowmelt and mud, alone and away from the corrals, he spun quickly enough to slip and go down and I came off of him, but held onto a rein somehow and then got back on. He finally grew calmer. We saved money to buy that borrowed trailer, and then a newer truck and we took a drive west to a national forest and rode the horses between boulders of granite and groves of aspen and we learned. Kelly's horse was calmer, a beautiful paint that had a heart of gold and it spooked at little, even when turkey vultures launched out of trees near the trail.

I called him Doc, after a blonde outlaw, Doc Scurlock, who rode with Billy the Kid. He wasn't much of an outlaw though, just a young horse with no experience ridden by a young man with less experience. But neither of us killed each other.

There is the horse. And then there is the ride. The trail ahead. And then there is another horse. There is always another horse. I rode

Doc for four years, up narrow trails, into tall mountains. On my first pack trip, I took him alone into the mountains with camp on his back while I led him on foot. I knew nothing of packing a horse, of balance—in my life or on the trail. But he tolerated these beginnings.

I rode him looking for elk. I rode him from Hawk's Rest on the Yellowstone down the river to Yellowstone Lake and back in a day, a distance of thirty-five miles. I rode him in an endurance ride and he won an award for best condition. I packed him in a long-pack string and disappeared into the mountains for two weeks. It was over his back that I learned how to tie the double diamond and the basket hitch.

During the winter, I plotted out future trips, dreaming of what lay ahead. And I rode that good yellow horse on those trails.

One day in late July, I sold the yellow gelding to a friend. I was getting horse-crazy then and found new ones to ride and train and I felt I had outgrown Doc. He had to go to a friend though, a home where I could keep in touch and even ride him now and then. He went to a man who had shown me the ropes—literally. On the morning that we went to load him into the horse trailer, he tore the lead rope out of my hands and galloped across the pasture to his herd. I caught him again and he did the same trick, this time dragging me part way. He knew. Eventually, we got him loaded and I watched the rump of my first horse fade into the distance as the horse trailer bounced up the dirt road. My first horse, my dream realized.

FOUR

Packing by the Book

—

I never met Joe Back. But I bet I would have liked him. And I would have liked to have thanked him.

I have never felt this to be truer than right now. Jim and I are in a deep hole of black timber just off the eastern rim of Red Mountain. There is a dead cow elk, my first elk, cooled off in the snow. Yesterday, as the last of the day eased by, I slipped up on an elk herd and shot a cow. By dark I had her cut up into quarters and made my way back up the mountain through the spruce and snow. Jim had a small campfire going when I got back to the old truck and its glow was a welcome sight. I was tired and worn. The next day, we would have an elk to take out, but that night we sat in Jim's home and ate fresh backstrap with gravy and drank whiskey and seven.

Bellies full, we mulled over our options which included walking down to the elk and packing her out on our backs, or getting permission to cross the East River through a big ranch. The East ran cold and clear and ice rimmed her banks, but it was a good option for two good horses like Todd and Mike. We made a phone call and now at midday, we are at the elk.

Jim digs in his saddle bags and pulls out a book, a thin blue and white book, *Horses, Hitches and Rocky Trails*, written by Joe Back in 1959. Tied behind the cantle on Jim's saddle is a hefty length of rope. I have a similar coil on mine. Last night, over our elk steak and whiskey, we hatched a plan: cross the river, ride up through the ranch, into the aspens and the spruce for five miles. At the elk, we would pack the quarters on our riding saddles and lead the horses out on foot. Much better than packing the elk out uphill to the truck. To pack the quarters on the elk, we would need a little bit of rope and a lot of technique. There, in Joe Back's book, was the technique. A way to sling a load on a riding saddle.

"Never tried it, but I'll bet we can figure it out."

The hitch comes slowly, with one of us holding the book and doing the instructing, while the other works the rope up and around the cantle, looping around the horn. The rope trails in the snow and freezes stiff and every once in a while, we step out from the shade where the elk quarters lie into the warmth of the sunlight.

He was a cowboy, Joe Back, but he was also an artist and a darned good one, trained at the Art Institute of Chicago. He ran strings of dudes into the mountains outside Dubois, Wyoming, during some of his career, but then he turned himself full-time to art. The book we are using was his classic, his *The Old Man and the Sea*. It is easy to use and full of wry humor and good illustrations. There's advice like these words for our effort: Tighten up your cinch and prepare to walk, buddy.

By late afternoon, we have hefted the quarters up onto the willing backs of Mike and Todd, and have started off down toward the ranch. We walk slowly at first, checking back on the loads, stopping once to check the tightness of rope, then on down. It feels good to be heading down, heading out with meat for the winter. I lead Mike, walking through the snow, easing down out of the high-country spruce to the aspens and sage, lost in thought, listening to the sounds of the horse behind me, the rustling of my pant legs against the dried grass and mule ear. Jim is ahead leading

49

Todd, the bay working gracefully down the trail, the hindquarters of the elk rocking back and forth on his frame. My friend carries his rifle in one hand, hoping to see an elk perhaps. I have a mule deer tag in my pocket, but I left my rifle at home, thinking only of packing, not of hunting. The trail is a good one, etching down off the mountain through the sagebrush and aspens, through a few wire gates and then down to the ranch and the pickup truck and trailer.

Suddenly, Jim stops in his tracks and turns to me in that hunched tiptoe of the hunter who has spotted game ahead. He turns to me like this, ducking down, his horse behind him.

"There's a nice buck standing up there at the edge of the aspens. Here, take my rifle, I'll tie up the horses."

I can see the buck and three does about two hundred yards off at the timber. The buck is staring at us and with one good leap, could be in the timber and gone. I drop to my stomach and ease up the rifle. I have never shot this rifle before, but my thumb finds the safety and when the crosshairs swing across the animal, I finger the trigger.

The horses stand there patiently, tied with elk quarters while we work in the wilting light of the day dressing out the big buck. I set aside the heart and liver and toss some old snow inside the body cavity, then cover the carcass with spruce boughs. Hopefully that will be enough to keep the coyotes off until we can come back up tomorrow morning.

At last light, we start down the mountain, watching the pink fade on the tips of the mountains across the valley, then the color dilutes out of everything and all is gray, then black. We work by feel and the cold comes up the river and through our wool jackets. It is utterly dark when we get to the river, which runs deep and cold in front of us. Going up in the morning, we had thought about having to cross that river on foot, leading horses, but the thought flitted quickly through our brains. Now we have the obstacle before us and the last thing we want to do is wade a cold river, even though the pickup truck is just a few hundred yards away in the ranch yard.

Elk on the saddle. Lead ropes in hand. Maybe we can scramble up onto the horses and ride behind the cantle, on the rump of the horse, across the river.

"Think they'll stand still for that?"

"We can only try I guess," said Jim. "I'm not too keen on the other option."

I'm remembering the first time I tried to get on Mike the traditional way, let alone from behind, riding on his rump, steering only with a lead rope. That was more than a year ago and I've ridden some trails since then, but still.

But it is dark and it is getting colder and the pickup truck is on the other side of the river. I get the big gray down off the riverbank and slither up behind the elk quarters and the saddle and we start off into the water. Behind me, Jim athletically launches onto Todd's rump and we both splash across, the horses calmly walking as if this happens every day. In only a few minutes, we are at the other side and the pickup truck is just a short walk away. My thoughts turn to elk steak and whiskey and to the next day. There's a good buck up there to pack off that mountain.

"Hey, Jim, better leave that book in your saddlebags."

FIVE

Dead Broke

—

Once in a great while, you will find a horse that seems to come out of the womb dead broke and ready to ride. Gabby is one of those horses. Calm, gentle Gabby.

We are heading out through a stand of thick whitebark pine, the horses' hooves punching through a crust of week-old snow. It is October and the smell and feel of the hunt is in the air. On this cold morning, we are going in to help a friend pack out of the high country. He's been back in there for a week with a buddy, hunting a tall basin, looking for elk. This is bighorn sheep country, steep and craggy and mostly open, but there are elk in here. They will probably have meat hung.

I have been trying to learn the art of packing. It is coming slowly, the hitches learned eagerly and practiced again and again. There seems to be a knack that comes only with time and experience, a way of going, measuring, balancing, and tying. On this trip, for me, it is mostly about the gear. I have some of the stuff, but not all of it. One pack saddle. An extra riding saddle. A lash rope or two. One set of panniers. A veteran looking at my gear would laugh me off the mountain. The panniers are especially ridiculous, for they are homemade out of plywood, thin-sided and varnished to a high sheen. They look pretty, but what they have in attractiveness they lack in volume and in durability. Hard-box panniers made of thin plywood do not last long in tough country.

"Those will make some nice kindling," a seasoned packer told me when he looked over my outfit. He was teaching me the diamond hitch and a little humility.

I had traded a Jeep for them, some cash and a rifle. The Jeep needed a lot of work and a new rear end, but I'm wondering if I got the better of the trade or not. I had not yet shot the rifle, but if the panniers are any indication, maybe I got taken. I make a vow to get rid of them as soon as I can. Perhaps make them into a coffee table.

Gabby has pack duty today, and she's wearing the riding saddle with nylon panniers that fit over the horn and cantle. If my friend has killed an elk, I can slip a hindquarter into each side and get it off the mountain.

The trail is steep and my saddle horse leans into it, pulling hard for the top. Gabby follows, barely tightening the lead rope in my right hand.

She was born in a southern Missouri pasture and she came into my life not according to plan. We had saved for years for the trip and with money in our account, we were going to purchase a new horse trailer from a manufacturer after driving from central Wyoming to Missouri. Then we would go horse shopping. After the horse trailer was purchased, we figured we'd have enough for one horse. We wanted a mare and a good one. We had two geldings already, but the idea of a colt or two on the ground was irresistible. With a good mare, we'd have that start.

Word of Gabby came as an afterthought. The rumor of a young filly of two and not very well-gaited. We thought we'd take a look.

The farmer was a soft-talking man who owned a good stud and seemed embarrassed, yet somehow proud of the gangly two-year-old out in his pasture. She was the slate blue color of a morning sky, with dark black legs and head. A blue roan. For some, this is the best color on a horse, a color that changes as the months slip by, that gets bluer with spring and darker with autumn.

"Pretty Gabby."

There was affection there, some pride. She stood watching our approach, standing out in a herd of sorrels and bays in a big pasture. Most of the herd moved off at our approach, but the young blue filly stood her ground, friendly. The morning sun slanted off the tall grass and already the muggy heat was on us. I thought about chiggers and such strange creatures as we walked out there, glad I was wearing boots and jeans. We'd dodged turtles on the country road to get here, and the occasional snake lying roadside like a black-curled section of rubber. A long way from Wyoming.

The farmer wore coveralls and a thin cotton t-shirt that had once been white, a sweat-salted ball cap. He walked around her and threw a lead rope over her head, tied it into a rein, and hopped on her bareback. She stood calmly and I looked over at my friend, Paul the horse-trader. He lifted his eyebrows. Easy to catch in a big pasture. Bareback on a two-year-old. There is that.

"She just isn't that well-gaited," said the farmer. The blue roan filly walked smoothly and her stride was long. The man pushed her up a notch and she swung into a longer trot, but you could see it there, the gait, hidden. The potential anyway. I looked over at Paul again. He smiled.

The price was right, but we'd spent most of our money on the horse trailer and on a beautiful bay mare from another farm. I looked at Paul again.

"She seems pretty nice. I love that color. Amazing."

"Oh, there's no bad color on a good horse."

"I just am a little bit short. Probably just enough money to get home."

The farmer was out of earshot.

"I'll lend you the money."

"I won't be able to pay you until next month."

"Not worried about it."

"Okay."

A day later, we loaded the two mares into the new trailer and headed west, back home, bucking a hot headwind through Nebraska, heading for cool Wyoming. We would get by now, for we had the land, a little piece of it anyway, and four horses. Our herd was growing. If we found a good stud somewhere, maybe we would raise some babies.

Now half the year has slipped by and young Gabby has been to the mountains. Several times. We switchback up the trail through the timber, hoof clinking on rock, the thick smell of snow and pine and horse. When we break out on the ridge, riding out of the black timber, the sun hits us full and good, and off in the distance the Owl Creeks and the Absarokas have risen, white shoulders in a perfect blue sky. South is the rest of the Wind River Range, canyons of rock and timber and basins filled with snow and ice. Up high, we can see plumes of snow kicking off the peaks, but the wind is there and not here.

The hunters have an elk down and they are glad to see us. Their camp has been tucked back into the mouth of a big ravine and it is cold down in there among the big old trees, coyoted out like that, eating freeze-dried food and working hard for warmth and for game. The game is a nice six-point bull and we heft the quarters up onto the back of my gentle young blue mare. My friend offers to pack the antlers out on his own and I'm glad that he does, for I can't remember the hitch I'd need to tie it on top of the load. This is the first time that Gabby has packed anything of any kind and I shake my head and think about how only a few months ago, she was in a pasture of waist-deep grass with a farmer on her bare back, more than a thousand miles from here.

We move out slowly, easing down off the ridge. I glance nervously back at the young blue horse several times, but she moves calmly, the load of elk meat swaying casually back and forth on her young narrow frame. Behind us trail our friends. Camp is on the other horse and my wife leads that one. This is the horse with the right gear, a pack saddle. But all rookies must make mistakes. She thinks I'm crazy for loving horses and mountains so much, but there is no turning back.

At the crest of the ridge, the trail dives off into the timber and the horses skid and slide, turning in switchbacks down the hill. A veteran packer with a few seasons under his belt might have checked the loads before moving down into the timber, but I am far from claiming such foresight. Once we are committed to the trail, there is no good place to stop and adjust a load until you are at the bottom.

The first sign of trouble comes halfway down.

"The saddle is riding up on Gabby."

I turn and see that the elk's hindquarters are nearly up to the young mare's shoulders, and the horn of the saddle is well up there, halfway up her neck. I dive off my saddle horse, leaving the reins trailing. Immediately, he starts to walk down the trail and I slip and slide on the steep slope, get him tied to a tree and move back to the pack horse.

There is no moving the saddle. I could unpack and repack, but the slope is so steep that I cannot move without falling down.

"We'll just have to go slow."

I get remounted and we move out very slowly, one step after another, down through the timber.

"The saddle is still coming up on her."

There's a nervousness in my gut, but there is no turning back. Were I to have a pack saddle, the britchen—a strap that reaches around the rump—would keep the saddle from sliding up. But on thin young horse without a pack saddle, the saddle slides right up onto the neck.

I start praying for the bottom, where the trail levels off before winding down through the sagebrush to the pickup truck. Maybe if we just go slower, but already the horses are going much slower than I could imagine any horse traveling. A walker-bound geriatric could make better time.

It goes like this for a while, the commentary coming from behind, the gradual slipping of the saddle up onto Gabby's neck, the thick panic in my stomach. Finally, after what seems like an eternal downward slide, we hit the bottom of the trail and I jump off my saddle horse, holding the lead rope in my hand, looking for a handy tree where I can tie Gabby and we can repack the load.

Before I can make the move, Gabby either decides she needs a bite of grass or the weight of all that elk steak on her ears is enough for her to drop her head. The load does one final, fateful slide, right up over the young blue mare's ears. In an instant, her head is pinned between her front legs, and there's more than one hundred pounds of elk meat holding it down. There's a thin scream from back up the trail, but I step around, grasp the off-side billet, give it a tug and Gabby raises her head, steps calmly backward, snorts, and is free of the saddle, elk meat and all. The makings of a world-class horse wreck disappear.

It takes us a while to repack and reload, but the young horse stands through it all. Finally we move off down through the sagebrush, toward the pickup truck. I'm thinking it's time to buy another packsaddle and wondering if I should send that farmer in Missouri a little more money for a young blue horse named Gabby.

SIX

On a Dark Horse

—

The black is tall and lean. His head is refined, jaw dish-shaped, neck arched perfectly. He gives those legs and that head to his colts and, if you breed him to a good round-hipped mare, you can balance out the fact that his hip is too flat. A rafter hip, but he doesn't throw it. He puts dandy colts on the ground.

He paces in his corral sometimes, smelling the mares out there in the pasture, and bellowing. Spring is still a few months off, but it is coming and even in February, there's a stirring in him. But still he is gentle.

A month ago, I took him out on the desert and we rode over drifts of cement snow with a friend who was not nearly as well-mounted. The friend was impressed by the dark horse, the way the stallion seemed to roll over the sagebrush sea, by the way he moved, but especially by his gentleness.

"You sure that horse has nuts?"

I laughed.

The black stud does that to people. A year ago, a lifetime ago, a couple came to see the dark horse in summer pasture. It was gin and tonic season and I was out on the porch sipping one, wearing shorts and flip-flops, basking in the Wyoming warmth that lasts not long enough. They wanted to see the stallion in action, under saddle, moving. He grazed placidly over the rim of my gin glass and I caught him with a halter, threw the rope over his neck, tied it off into a makeshift single rein and hopped on him bareback. Still in flip-flops and shorts. I was tempted to ask for my cocktail, but didn't. He trotted. Cantered, spun. Walked. Turned. They watched, thanked me and left. I let him go back to grazing and was back to the porch before my ice melted.

The horse does in fact sport testicles, and physical proof stands in two good colts out in the meadow, tugging at dead-of-winter grass. They have his head, his long-tall conformation, his way of going. Most importantly, his disposition. He's been packed and picketed and he's been ridden on the trail alongside mares. I call him Ace, although this is not his registered name. In the spring he gives me colts and hope with the brilliance of a green pasture. But now it is winter and all the big black stud and I share is a sense of longing.

This February, darkness has swept across my world, enough to clog my thoughts. Woman trouble. She and I are splitting up our stuff and in the end, I'll keep a just pickup truck and a horse or two. The black stud will be one of those and I look at him now out there in that small corral and think it's time to get out on the land, out on the rolling desert. It has been a gloomy winter, the skies choked with gray clouds that offer no snow. The country around town is wide open and snowless, but the skies are thick and close. Threatening. It seems to have been this way forever, the weeks dragging by, the sky dark, the land thirsty for moisture. And nothing changes.

This morning I rise to coffee and pain and I hear that dark horse out there. It is time to ride, time for big country. Today, though the skies offer no hint of sun, the land calls me.

I catch the big black horse and talk to him, throw my saddle up on his good withers and load him into the horse trailer. He moves without complaint and we bounce up the long rough road out to the highway. South of town is a huge chunk of public land where you can ride forever across adobe badlands and little clumps of sagebrush cling to a mean soil. The grass between the clumps is pathetic. The soil, though, is good for a barefoot horse, for there are only a few rocks. In a wet year, it's a quagmire that causes your horse to slip and stumble and if you're foolish enough to drive out into that gumbo, you will sink your vehicle down to the doorframe and pray for a hard freeze. Now, though, it is dry and perfect for riding.

Hank is with us too—lean, fit Hank, all muscle and hide, a hard-charging white setter with as much grace and style as the dark horse. He's been there, up the mountain, out in the desert, in the Dakota pheasant fields and on the wind-washed desert chukar partridge cliffs. Ace and Hank and me. I laugh at this as I shut off the diesel and lead Ace out of the horse trailer. Three fellas out for a ride. All of us with a little too much testosterone for our own good.

I swing up and Hank charges out in the lead, out into the gray sweep of the winter desert. I walk Ace for a while, lost in thought, thinking about life and transitions and forgiveness. This sticks on me for a while as I listen to the big stallion's hooves on the clay. Hank gallops back occasionally, panting madly, checking in, then charging off until he is just a white speck out there. The dog is a prisoner of his nose, and he follows it into the light breeze, looking for sage grouse.

He finds them eventually, miles up the two-track road that we've been following. I see him out there, frozen like a statue, his tail out stiff, one front leg cocked. I press the reins against the black stud's neck and we turn toward the dog, cantering in to where he has the grouse pinned down. Sage chickens are spooky and it is the rare dog that does not flush them wild. Hank is that dog. As we come up to him, I see him glance briefly our way, not turning his head, but raising his eyebrows as if to say, "Right here, what the hell is taking you so long?"

I step off the saddle horse and walk in, holding the reins in my hand. Out in front of Hank, a flock of at least forty sage chickens takes to the air. The reins tighten in my hand as Ace throws his head up at the flush, but he does not spook. I watch the big birds fly off over the land, huge gray grouse fading into the flat monotone canvas of the sagebrush ocean and then they are gone. They gather like this in the winter, big groups. I've seen one hundred or more in one flock out here.

Perhaps, for him, there is safety and comfort in numbers. I am the opposite. I find solace in the landscape, the aloneness. The stallion and the stud dog are comfort enough for me. For now.

Hank gallops frantically over the patch of hard clay and sagebrush where the flock stood, then slams to a sudden stop and another point and then two more sage grouse get up and fly off, chasing the big flock into the western sky. They flap and soar. Flap, flap, flap, soar. And they are gone. They have faded into the far horizon and all I see now is the whiteness of the snow-blanketed Wind River Range against the somber sky. I mount the big horse again, stretching my leg high for the stirrup, swinging up and following the white dog out into the world.

We work toward the 'dobes, hills of clay piled out on the sagebrush, molded by wind and water. They rise several hundred feet above the flat, like dirty foam on a snowmelt stream. I turn the stud up one long thin ridge and he pulls hard for the top, leaning into the breast collar, huffing, chugging up the hill. On both sides, the ridge falls away steeply to a ravine choked with rabbitbrush, greasewood, and sage. When we crest the ridge, Hank is on point again at the very tip of the draw. He points downward, into the head of the steep ravine and there lies a big buck mule deer, rack thick and dark against the adobe background. He stares up at Hank and the dark horse and then he is on his feet and jumping down the draw, clearing twenty, twenty-five feet in each bound, putting distance between us. Then he is gone. I hear the thumping of his retreat, the clatter of a rock and silence.

At noon, we make the mushroom rocks, way out in the desert, well beyond the sounds of town and people. There is no one out today, not even a motorcyclist. The rocks are a beacon, a lighthouse on the sagebrush sea. The clump of sandstone spires rise out of a southern sagebrush-cloaked ridge, rising as high as forty feet above. Their bases are pure white, soft sandstone, but their caps are darker. Atop some of the mushrooms lichen and sagebrush grow and in a fork between two rocks is the thick rough nest of some kind of raptor. The rocks stretch for only a couple of acres, but on a good day from a high ridge, you can see them out there in the desert from miles away. It's a good halfway point, a place to rest before you turn back. If you travel right and the day is good, you will have taken a day to do this ride. I do not know how far it is out here, but our pace has been slow and steady. A walk. Sometimes a trot.

The sun is out, but I do not remember when it appeared. I turn my eye to the sky and I realize that the clouds are gone. Somehow I missed that, lost in thought, watching the dog, feeling the horse beneath me. Up against the rocks it is warm and I shed a jacket, pull some saddle hobbles from the saddle bags and leave Ace hobbled at the base. I sit back against stone. Hank twirls in a circle up against my left leg and lies down, panting and happy, while the big black horse moves off a few feet and nibbles at a clump of poor grass. My hand finds the dog's soft big head and I rest it there for a time and then I turn to the saddlebags. I dig out a chunk of elk salami and smoked gouda and an apple. I share the core with Ace and sit back in the sun, dozing occasionally. The thick, dark thoughts that caught up with me this morning are gone and now I lean against a crumbling sandstone spire and listen to my dog panting and my horse munching and there is not much else there.

I wonder if perhaps Theodore Roosevelt had a moment like this and think that likely he did. His pain was greater than mine, a pain thick and black and final. In the same house, on the same day—Valentine's Day for God's sake—his twenty-two year-old wife and his mother died only hours apart. When his bride Alice died in his arms shortly after his mother's death, he was left with an infant daughter and a giant hole in his heart. He purged, burning things, throwing other things away. "The light has gone out of my life," he wrote. He destroyed everything that reminded him of Alice and it has been said that after the funeral, he never spoke her name again.

He found a good horse and a western badlands landscape of sandstone and sagebrush flung out to the far horizon. He rode and shot his rifle and he was better. Then he went home from North Dakota and became President of the United States. Found another woman. Had children. Adventures. Lived life. A full life. Laughed. Loved. Rose above it. Maybe it seemed like the end to him back then, but open country and a horse—especially the horse—cured it. There's a picture of him that I've seen atop a dark horse on his Dakota ranch, all dressed out in buckskins with a rifle in his hand. Later in his life, when the stress of living in the White House was too much, he saddled a big athletic horse named Bleistein and galloped through Rock Creek Park, randomly snapping pistol shots at trees, leaping over downed logs, splashing across streams, spooking pedestrians. Riding away from it all in the middle of Washington, D.C.

Astride a horse, a man feels like more than himself. A greater thing. Bigger, larger. The horse is large enough to absorb your pain and on a good horse, there are no dark thoughts that you can't out-ride on a long day.

They do it to us, those good creatures. It has been said that the outside of a horse is good for the inside of a man and on this warm winter day with my back up against a rock that has been carved by a generation of wind, I think that there is absolute truth in the statement. One does not even have to be mounted for the horse to dilute and heal. Walk into the pasture and throw your arms around a good horse's neck. Bury your face in the mane. Smell that good pungent odor of horse hair. Breathe deeply. Or just watch them out there on a high ridge, grazing in the fading sunlight of a long summer's day. They are high enough on that slope to catch a breeze that keeps the bugs down and their tails swish only occasionally, they shake their manes between every third step as they go grass-clump to grass-clump across the skyline. Watch them closely and later you will realize that is all you have been doing. Watching. No thinking. In the moment and the horses have been all. Just watching and all other thoughts have been somewhere else.

And then there is the feeling you get when a young horse hits the ground for the first time and he struggles to his feet and finds his mamma's teats and you laugh at how his mouth puckers and a loud slurping sound dominates the open air of the corral. You laugh, too, when he scampers in the pasture and kicks and leaps. Those are the good thoughts that a horse brings to a human. Their outside is indeed good for our inside.

There are those among us who do not feel this way, who feel disconnected, scared perhaps, when encountering horses. I wonder if their roots, their ancestors, were foot people, trudgers. If this is so, mine were born horseback. There is no place I would rather be than on a good horse with miles ahead.

The horse and the dog seem to operate on another plane than me, a higher plane, one where their world is the land, food, sex, my company. On this winter day, I look for that place, for that level and they get me there, somehow. Their company alone, their acceptance of me as me, and nothing more.

I catch up the big horse and slip the bit back into his mouth, twist the stirrup in my hand and find it with my boot. Then I am up there, and the view is better, bigger, brighter. Hank thunders off into the sagebrush and I turn Ace to follow him.

We walk at first and then I feel the roar of black thoughts coming up behind me, of the logistics of a divorce, of things said and done and not said and not done. Of mistakes that you did not know were mistakes until you looked backward over months and years with the bias of hindsight. Of things too close to see, like trying to focus on your palm, trying to read the lines in your hand when it is only an inch from your face and then, finally, straightening your elbow until your palm is out there and you can see every line. Distance and time. Space.

But the space for me now is open country, miles of it and as those dark images come up, I boost the big stud up into a trot and then into a canter. We are following an old jeep trail out across the flats. It rises on a wave of sagebrush, up a long ridge. Off in the distance, against the western skyline is Wind River Peak, smothered in snow, shining brightly in the sun. I can almost imagine spring coming to the land, an optimistic thought. I canter the black. He moves easily and gracefully, so smooth it feels as if I am in a rocking chair, or better yet, on my porch swing back home, sans gin and tonic. But this is tonic enough, this long gait, this gentle movement.

The hooves drum on the soft clay and Ace exhales in tempo and then Hank is beside us, cantering to his own beat, in perfect time to Ace's movements. The sun is on my arms and my back and it is warm and right. We do this for a mile, then walk, then trot, then up to a lope again, occasionally a gallop. But mostly the canter and the rocking chair. The dog, the stallion, and a man. And in that moment I realize that everything is going to be all right.

SEVEN

Big as the Mountain

—

Dawn. Elk are talking on the mountain and I have no way to talk back. I have left my best elk bugle back in the truck and the truck is six miles away. Six miles of stream bottom and willow patch, six miles winding down a canyon over cobblestone. With elk on the mountain, it might as well be a hundred.

But I have no choice. I work fast on cold leather stiff with frost. I brush out the big gray, throw a blanket rigid with yesterday's sweat up onto his long back, and then work the saddle in place. He is a mountain of a horse. My head is just a few inches above the top of his withers. Seventeen full hands of horse. Big, fast horse. I pull the cinch tight, then spin the gray down into a shallow trough in the mountain meadow. He is so tall that any height advantage you can take is a good idea and it is best to put this horse in a hole to get on him. I swing up in one quick motion. Big Lad steps into the bit and I hold him back, nod at my hunting partner, who is already heading up the mountain after the elk, and turn down the trail.

Lad is a veteran, a horse that has been up and down this trail a dozen times. I need that elk bugle, for superstitious reasons, if for nothing else. How can I take an elk without an elk bugle that has been responsible for calling in dozens of bulls? I have other bugles, but there is only one lucky bugle. Elk hunters are like that sometimes. Patterned, ritualistic, strange.

So I turn the big gray horse for the trailhead, away from his buddies in camp, away from a day of rest and into a morning of work.

It is a calm, cold morning and the willows are thickly frosted and there's a pane of ice at every stream crossing. Lad crashes through without hesitation, swinging in that big walk of his, up the far side, stepping out, moving easy. My only job is to hold him in for he would canter if he could and my left arm is cocked hard against the reins and already getting sore with the strain of holding eleven hundred pounds of horse into a reasonable gait. It is cold enough that I tuck my chin down into my jacket, and pull my hat down over my ears. My fingers and toes are cold, but I can only tough it out.

The trail narrows into a thick stand of lodgepole, crossing the stream again, and I see the tracks of elk in the frost. Fresh tracks, but even they do not deter me from my mission. I've shot many elk without that bugle, but logic has nothing to do with it. I ride to the tap of horse hooves on frozen September mud and then we break out into a big meadow and there's a bull moose standing in the willow, steaming in the cold air, looming above the yellow forest of leaves. He swings his head our way, a big rack of antlers swaying, catching the first glint of morning sunlight. He moves off, nose held high, jogging up out of the creek bottom and into the thick timber on the far side. Lad pays no attention.

Up out of the meadow onto a bench, following the stream as it carves a tiny canyon, then diving down off into it, following the trail. We have seen no one on this opening morning, but as we get closer to the trailhead, I round a bend and see two hunters on foot, rifles slung. They see the big gray coming, head swaying, stepping out, and they step off the trail, watching, nodding, and saying hello.

"Nice looking horse."

"Thanks."

I do not stop to chat. I am focused and the big gray wouldn't stand for it anyway, he'd spin on the trail and stomp and paw. A goer. Lad always gets a word or two, no matter where I go. A big gray horse like that, one that can walk forever, gets a compliment even from people on foot. Or maybe especially from people on foot. I imagine it's hard to look at horse and rider and not envision a scenario that has you in the saddle. Especially when that horse is a traveling horse.

At the truck, I tie Lad and give him some grain while I dig out the truck keys and find the bugle. It takes about fifteen minutes and then I'm back on Lad again.

This time, the big horse soars over the ground. The rest of the horse herd is back up the trail and he knows it and he's moving in one of the best, smoothest, ground-eating gaits in the world. Splashing through the stream, the ice now melted in the morning sun, we zip through stands of willow, the frost turned to dew, and the toes of my hunting boots wet with it. Lad climbs the canyon without hesitation, moving fast and easy and not slowing even on the steepest stretches of trail. Going. Moving. Upward. The wind whistles in my ears and it is just from the locomotion of the horse alone, for it is dead calm. A ruffed grouse scurries ahead of the hooves and bursts into the air for a short flight, landing in a trail-side spruce. On. Fast.

There is no sign of the moose in the big meadow, but there are fresh black bear tracks in the mud at the last stream crossing, only a few hundred yards from camp. The big gray nickers to his friends as we come out of the stand of timber and into the small meadow where camp is. We are back. The ride has taken two hours, up and back, half the time it takes when we ride in slowly with pack horses. When I pull off the saddle and blanket, the back of the big gray is just damp and in minutes, I have hobbles on him and he's out with his buddies, head down, work done. Not bad for a horse nearing his twenty-second year and almost completely blind in his right eye.

I have a mountain of my own to climb and elk to talk to.

Two winters ago, the snow lay deep on the pasture and the big gray horse turned his butt to the bruising wind. It was a real winter for a change, an old-fashioned winter, with cold, stinging snow on a west wind and hay blown open and green across a canvas of brilliant snow. That morning, Lad stood off by himself. Not like him. And I went to the big horse and saw his right eye, and saw a cloud there like smoke boiling out of a ditch bottom during spring burn.

The veterinarian said the blindness had not been caused by injury. He worked with the horse for a while and determined that perhaps he could see just a bit with the right. The left was still fine. I thought about a horse that couldn't see in his right eye and I thought about all those trails where one misstep is one too many. I thought about that big gray horse. He had been the anchor, the herd boss, the one that you could always rely on, a horse built for the high country.

Lad did everything big: his mountain walk, his confidence, his attitude. For a saddle horse, he was a massive animal, a full and honest seventeen hands. This was the way a horse was supposed to be put together. Nothing about him was out of proportion.

Lad had been the personal horse of a horse trader, a tall, lean friend named Paul who sported a thick crop of white hair and talked softly. Here was a man who bought horses by the trailerful, who had laid eyes on every horse in the country and had bought and sold horses like one might buy eggs at the grocery. He rarely owned one more than a year before it found a new home. Paul owned Lad for seventeen.

He had purchased the big gray as a three-year-old, and from the start, the horse had been a go-to horse, the kind of animal that can quickly intimidate a lesser horseman. But Paul is a horseman and after a year of training, he had Lad worked out and smoothed down. Later in Lad's career, he turned into the kind of horse that you could ride in parades, and still later, put a beginner on. But as a young horse, only Paul was confident enough to ride a horse that traveled like that and had the fire.

By the time I bought Lad for a bargain price, he was nineteen, past his prime, but with rivers yet to cross and mountains to climb. Paul didn't want to watch the old gray go down, withering away as horses are prone to do until they are swaybacked husks of bone and hide and gums. My string of saddle horses was young and I needed a veteran to lead the way. He had been up the mountain, this mountain of a horse, and that was what I needed more than anything. A horse with the confidence to lead.

When I picked him up, he hopped right in the trailer without a moment of hesitation. He was like that, a horse with no stop. He had one annoying habit. He wanted to go. And because he wanted to go, he pawed. Constantly. If he was tied, he wasn't happy. At road heads, he would paw the ground impatiently as other horses were packed and saddled. He'd paw in the trailer while he waited for other horses to load. I started putting him in last, for he'd hop right in, shoving smaller horses out of his way, ready for the ride.

The day I brought him home, traveling several hundred miles of back roads from western Colorado to central Wyoming, he pawed the whole way. I'd feel him back there, rocking the trailer from side to side, stomping about. Unhappy. When I got to town, I stopped off at my local watering hole, put a bucket of grain in with Lad, and went in for a beer. When I came out, I found that Lad had overturned the bucket and pawed it into plastic shrapnel.

In his prime, Lad had been a stunning dapple gray like the horse that Clint Eastwood rode in *Pale Rider*, but by the time he came into my life, he was white.

"What's with that big white horse?" people asked. "Wow, he's really something."

People in the horse breeding business asked why he had been gelded. Many times. Later, I traced down his original owner and found out that he had been a handful as a young colt, unruly. Once he'd been in an indoor arena at the Missouri horse farm where he was raised. He'd been tied while the trainer was off doing something else, but had come untied somehow and made his way in the open door to the farm's business office. There, the colt rounded several office chairs and a desk cleanly without havoc, but he'd smashed a single light bulb on the ceiling. Even as a two-year-old, he was tall enough to scrape the ceiling. The trainer started calling him Light Bulb. Then someone made the unwise decision to geld him and those amazing genes were taken out of the breed. Years later, the old gelding found his way into my horse herd. I kept a stud then, a big black, and when breeding season was on,

Lad would go crazy, for he thought he could do the job even if he couldn't. His job, though, was to anchor a herd of young horses, providing them with confidence, but also providing confidence to less experienced riders.

He stepped out with the strength of horses half his age. He was a combination of speed and assurance often sought but rarely found in mountain horses. Lad had it. For this reason, he was often at the head of the pack string with a rookie on his back.

From way up there, you gained confidence. The horse had so much of it that it filtered right into you. Though it was often beginners who found themselves on Lad's back, accomplished riders appreciated his drive. One summer, six of us took a trip deep into the Absarokas, entering one end of the wilderness and coming out at another. It was a week-long affair, with a bunch of horses of all ages. Only a few hours into the trip, we came to a high bridge across the South Fork of the Buffalo. I couldn't get my horse to cross the bridge and the young pack horse I was leading only made it worse. Other saddle horses refused as well. Mark, a friend who was a skilled rider, was on Lad.

"Put Lad across that bridge," I told him.

The rest of the trip, the big old horse was in the lead, stepping out, heading down the trail in that ground-eating stride of his.

Later, when we crossed the deep, cold Thorofare River, all of us except Mark on Lad got wet feet.

One September, another friend took Lad by himself and rode all day on a rough trail as he scouted far away from camp. He arrived at dusk that evening, tired, yet sated with the feel of a good horse and a good day.

"That's a hell of a horse. That's a hell of a horse."

It was about all he could say that night. I remember that moment as one in which Dave changed from a learning rider to a confident, competent horseman.

Fittingly, we were back in the mountains when I noticed that his left eye was starting to cloud a bit too. It was at elk camp and the old horse had done his duty and was grazing contentedly with his herd out in the meadow. I rode him a bit that trip, but not much. Once, he stumbled and fell to his knees at the edge of a deep ravine. It scared me and it scared him.

After that hunt, I started to make him my personal horse, for I was afraid he might hurt a rider who wasn't ready for the unexpected. In his final years, his sole purpose was to carry me up and down the mild trail to elk camp each September. The hard work of packing elk out of the high tough places was left to younger horses that hadn't yet paid their dues.

In elk camp, I didn't even bother with hobbles for Lad. He moved out there in the dark, never far from the mares, white, luminous, visible even on the blackest night. He was content to hang out in the meadow, coming in for grain or to have his butt scratched now and then. He stood with his butt to you and you scratched. Then you stepped aside, and he'd shift position to have his butt scratched again. It was laughable. You could get him to turn a complete circle with that itch.

Last fall, I rode him up and down the trail at least a half dozen times as we took three elk out of the mountains. He moved as he always did, never stopping, never hesitating. Always trusting.

A few months later, while he was enjoying his retirement with another old horse on a friend's ranch at the base of the big mountain south of town, he went blind. I went out to see him and it took my breath away. Now the big horse tentatively felt his way around the pasture, bumping into things, tripping on sagebrush, blundering into the barbwire. I knew that I had to make that decision.

And I knew, no matter what else, that a mountain horse should rest on the mountain, feeding the eagles and the coyotes, not buried in the landfill next to somebody's worn-out refrigerator.

Yesterday, with the warmth of the spring sun heavy in the pasture, Dave and I took Lad for one last walk. The ground had thawed and Lad was blind. I loaded him into the horse trailer and took him out to the base of the mountain, back up against the foot of it where greening grass chased the melting snow. A fox sprinted up the draw and over the hill as we arrived.

Lad ate a bait of grain and I marveled at how good he looked. This was not the aging rack of bones of most ranch and mountain horses nearing their twenty-fourth birthday. He was still regal, still strong and proud. But he could not see. After it was over, I burned those brand papers and some sage. And we smoked a cigar and talked of the big horse that made us all feel a little bigger and better.

EIGHT

Mountain Lady

—

There exists, inside a very few horses, a homing instinct. This is not the bad habit of "smelling the barn" and charging back home after a long day's ride. This is something much deeper, much closer to extrasensory, and much more useful. It is the ability to recognize a trail that has been tracked before, to remember where the turns and kinks are, and to make all the right moves, even on moonless nights or in the throes of whiteout blizzards that blot out sky and earth. It's a horse's inner GPS system. It's a surreal business and if you've ever ridden a horse like this, ever felt that the horse knew exactly what it was doing when you didn't have a clue, then you have felt that knot in your stomach, that thrill tingling in your spine and raising the hair on the backs of your arms while you let that horse do its thing. It's a wow moment that transcends any woodsmanship you may feel you have, that goes deeper and further than any training in orienteering, that is beyond man and lives only in animal and in one animal in particular. When this realization sweeps across your fabric, you know that you are merely a passenger and it's best to just hang on and to enjoy the view, for any thread of common sense you may bring to the picture will just interfere with something that is primal and real and unreal all at once.

I've had a couple of horses that could loosely remember trails on the backtrack. If you held a loose rein and made no attempt to turn them one way or another, they'd usually make the right turn, especially if they had walked up that same trail that same day. If you have a horse like this, hang on to him, because that is a trait worth money. Or if you are going to sell him, mark up the price. But if you have a horse like Jade, then no horse buyer's wallet can be fat enough.

I bought Jade from a backwoods Missouri farmer many years ago. His farm felt like something out of the thirties or forties, a little place perched on the side of a hill, with a confusing tangle of outbuildings and chicken pens. Horses stood hock-deep in mud and manure and I thought I heard banjo music coming from the house. Maybe I was overreacting, but we were deep in the Ozarks horse buying and I was feeling pretty far from the Wyoming mountains.

Jade stood tied to a hitching rail—the farmer knew we were coming—left hind cocked lazily. The farmer had taken the time to knock some of the dried mud and horse shit off of her coat and hit her with some bug spray. She looked like a gem. Jade was four years old at the time and I was impressed by her small frame, her fine features and head, her attitude. Before I bought her, I rode her down the lane while cicadas sang from the humid shade of oak and locust trees, listening to her small feet tapping on the hardpan in perfect rhythm. I bought her, and I think the farmer knew he was losing a good one, for he winced before he agreed to the price and he turned quickly from the trailer after we had Jade aboard. He didn't count the money. Sometimes, when I'm flush with cash from some writing job or another, I think I should send him another thousand dollars, but even that would not be enough. When the banks come for me, I'll sell every stick of furniture, everything I own, everything but Jade. She is the kind of animal that you can climb aboard in the spring and disappear into the mountains until winter. She will get you home.

Right from the start, she was a go-to gal. When I stepped out of the barn with a bridle in my hand, she came up to see what was going on, asking to go for a ride. In the spring, we hosted an annual pig roast and it wasn't unusual to look up from basting the hog to see four or five kids on Jade, bareback with only a halter. She was a natural.

In the mountains, she walked with the same attitude, ears forward, stepping out, going down the trail.

The first time I discovered her true worth was on a snowy cold October day high in the Wind River Mountains south of Dubois. A friend had asked me to help him get an elk camp in. He was hiking and wanted my horses to carry his camp. It was a long way in, up a cold ridgeline trail into the tall country. He wanted to camp high on the shoulder of a big mountain, where the elk came out to feed in the dim light of dawn before whispering back up the mountain. I agreed to help him, although I was new to horsepacking and riding mountain trails alone. So the friend walked in while Jade took care of me.

By the time we climbed more than a thousand feet to the base of the mountain where he would set up his elk camp, it was snowing hard and sideways. I tucked my chin down into my wool jacket, pellets of hard snow bouncing off my exposed cheek. The snow coated the windward side of Jade, hammering a sheet of white onto her hide, mane, and tail. She looked like a half-white, half-bay pinto cleaved by color lengthwise right down the middle rather than a bay lady with a lot of class. But she kept going into the sting of wind-driven snow. I could scarcely breathe as the wind ripped across my mouth and nose. Finally, we made camp and I quickly unloaded the packhorse and turned around in the saddle. "Good luck, I'll be back in a week."

Darkness was coming down and the wind had drifted in our back trail. I had left their camp at the edge of a meadow that gave way to timber on the north slope and a wide, white slope on the south side. The trail had come down that wide-open slope, but I couldn't find it. Everything looked the same. White. Jade kept tugging one way while I was certain that the trail was another. Finally, I gave up and let her have her head. Snow fell thickly across my gloves and arms and I was cold to the core. I didn't have the energy to argue.

She knew exactly where she was. Immediately, we were on the trail and in places where sagebrush blocked some wind, I could see faint traces of our tracks, blown in and disappearing quickly. There was no way I could find the trail, but she walked down the high ridge where it ran as if she were clicking her heels down that country road back home in Missouri. The trail was a rocky number, winding through Douglas fir and lodgepole pine and whitebark pine country near timberline. On a good day, it was a bad trail, but I tucked my head back into my jacket and let her go.

Where the trail bent, she bent, where the trail zigged, she zigged. At the crest of the ridge, the trail—which was really nothing more than an old outfitters route that followed the quickest and not necessarily the easiest way into the mountains—dove off into a steep slope of switchbacks that ran out at the bottom of the mountain. Jade never hesitated and I just held onto the reins and let her do the walking. At times it was more of an extended, but controlled skid with her hind legs tucked beneath her belly and her forelegs out, bracing, skidding, dropping downward through the ice-plated timber. Snow built up on my jacket, on Jade, and on the trees. In the blinding snow, I could barely see her ears, but she kept moving. We got back to the truck and trailer about an hour after dark. I brushed ice off her coat and loaded up for home, only just starting to understand her otherworldliness.

Two years later, I again reveled in her ability to find her way out of a tight spot with no help from her rider.

The country that lies south of Yellowstone National Park is about as wild as anything gets in Wyoming. It's a land of big rivers and vast slopes of timber. It is home to elk and grizzly, moose and wolves. It's big country and it calls to a person who has a bit of the wild country in his veins. If you ride up here on a light-struck blue day, far up the flanks of the mountain, you'll get what a friend of mine calls a Wyoming buzz. To the south is the high mesa of the Buffalo Plateau, white with the first snow of September and farther south and a click east are the crags of the Gros Ventre. North are the northern Absarokas and the Trident, and still farther north and west, you can see all the way into Montana and the Gallatins, tall above the carpeted forest plateau that is Yellowstone. In all that sweep of wide country, the roads and highways are few, the people fewer, and Wyoming aplenty.

On the southeastern end of this country, just before the mountains fall off into the valley of the Snake River, there are a few obscure peaks. These are mountains that will never be destination points for mountaineers, or photo points for professional cameramen.

But an elk hunter looking out over this country will feel his heart skip a beat or two. Threads of whitebark twist down off the mountains, blanketing the northern slopes. The southern slopes stand knee-deep in grass and wildflowers and the backsides of the mountains offer escape and hiding cover. On one side, the mountain slopes fade gently into open glades etched by cold streams, with pockets of green and fire-charred timber. This is game country.

When you see these mountains, you daydream about walking up there some evening with nothing but a sleeping bag, a flashlight, and a good rifle in the hopes of catching a big bull or buck at day's first blush. At the base of the mountain, at the right time of year, you will walk into a wet mountain corner at the top of a drainage and find signs of great destruction, as if something savage and angry has torn into the land. Wallows of mud, torn trees bleeding fresh sap, and the reek of elk piss will tell you that you have arrived in Elk Mecca.

One late September day, my friend Jim and I found one of these places. Above, we could glimpse the open ridges and streams of timber. We walked quietly back away from where we had tied the horses in the shade of an alpine fir. It was a hot afternoon, and the depths of the wet meadow where the bull elk had taken his mud bath felt cool and clean. We sat there for a time, imagining being here when that bull had been, watching him thrash the trees and tear up the sod with his big antlers. Then we moved up the mountain, walking slowly and listening.

As the day cooled and the mountain swallowed the sun, we heard a bull elk call from high on the slope, perhaps a thousand feet above us. I had a bugle and I answered back, and he answered me back and we climbed. We talked like this for a while, that bull and I, and we climbed while he dropped. Finally, far up the mountain and miles from our horses, the bull stepped out into the golden splash of the day's end. I can see him there, buckskin hide and shaggy dark mane, burned onto my memory. Jim pulled up his rifle.

It was dark by the time we returned to the horses, our hands smelling of elk blood, our bones tired. We were still many miles from camp and the trail below us was one of the ugliest we'd ever been on. It was a forgotten trail, a side route off the main thoroughfare that had been neglected for years by trail maintenance workers. In 1988, the fires that torched Yellowstone scoured through and took out many trees along the old trail. In its wake, the fire had left outstanding hunting, but poor riding. The carcasses of all those dead trees lay across the trail for miles. In the daylight, you had a hard time winding your way up through the deadfall, going around giant fallen trees, and spending more time off the trail than on it. The trees that had not fallen yet were charred black and white, skeletons with branches that threatened to remove an eye. Now we had to ride through all of that.

In the darkness, I spoke softly to my traveling mare and ungloved my hand long enough to rub it across her warm muzzle and fumble with the cold lead rope. I turned off my flashlight and swung up, in the lead. She stepped out, completely confident although there was no moon, no light. She moved down through the timber and although she had never been on the trail before that day, she made the moves. In each place where the trail went off into the brush to go around an obstacle, she stepped perfectly, almost as if treading in her own prints from the morning's ride. In the blackness, she stepped out and I pulled my hat down, tucked my chin in and prayed I wouldn't be leaving an eyeball on one of those branches.

It was an amazing ride. Even now, I can still feel that power, still feel that confidence that rose from that little mare as she moved out and headed down. Once, I turned on a flashlight, somehow stupidly thinking that she needed the help, and she immediately lost the trail for about a hundred yards. I shut the light back off and she found the trail again. Jim, riding behind me, saw sparks fly from horseshoe on rock, and the dim lights of Jackson far off to the south. Where the trail met the main, she turned and in minutes we were in camp, back home.

I do not know what it is about riding the back trail on the right horse. Do they smell their way? Is it memory? Sight? All of these?

Two years later, I happened to be riding Jade on the main trail, headed up country. When I got to the junction where the rough old side trail staggered off into the deadfall, Jade immediately turned up it with no reining from me. Perhaps she read my mind. She just turned. Fortunately, that's where I wanted to go anyway. The deadfall was still there and more had joined it. But the horse knew where she had gone around the snags two years before and all I had to do was stay on. She remembered.

Homing instinct set in, although that in and of itself does not make a good mountain horse. Calmness in the face of a potential horse wreck is the most important trait of all. It is a quality that some horses have and some do not.

But calmness is also an inherent trait, one that goes straight to the bone. In my mountain gal, steady is her middle name.

For many years, I camped for a week or more at the bottom end of a wide meadow deep in the Absaroka Mountains of north-western Wyoming. Here, for an all-too-brief time, I set up an elk camp, hunting with two brothers named Dave and Al. We walked out of this camp with our rifles, hunting thick timber, climbing distant ridges, sweating up tangled canyons. It was good to be there, to be alive in a September mountain meadow tinted with woodsmoke from the wall tent, hearing an elk bugle back in the timber up the mountain. There is no better place in the world to have a backcountry experience, for the land has grizzly and black bears, moose, elk, mule deer, coyotes, and wolves. It's like no other place on earth.

One fall, Dave and I rode into the meadow for a week's worth of hunting. It had been a good year, for I had killed a nice mountain sheep on another ridge far to the north. Now, we came into elk camp with that deep-down feeling of contentment, knowing that if we failed to take an elk out of these hills, it would be okay. If you camp in a place long enough and often enough, it starts to feel like home. The place on Pilgrim Creek felt that way.

Late that night, as we sat around the campfire, preparing for another hunt the next morning, we heard a surreal sound coming from back in the trees. It was a gurgling grunt that we couldn't identify, as if some hairy Sasquatch was coming into our camp, calling to us from the black timber. The hair rose on the back of my neck.

"Unnnuka."

Dave looked at me, eyes wide in the firelight. "What the hell is that?"

"Christ, I don't know."

"It's getting closer."

"Did you ever see the *The Blair Witch Project*?"

"Cut it out."

"Unnnuka!"

"It *is* getting closer."

"I've got the bear spray."

"Hey, I think I can make that noise. 'Unnnuka.'"

"Knock that shit off, it's coming into camp."

The sound circled us, then faded into the trees.

Dave gave it another try: "Unnnuka."

"Hey, damnit, you are calling it right into camp."

"I think it's a moose."

It was. A bull moose, with antlers like the cattle catcher on an old locomotive. He looked as big as a train too. He came closer in the darkness of the meadow and we stepped to the edge of the lodgepole pines, away from the fire and shined our flashlights out into the darkness. There, on the end of her picket rope, was Jade staring face-to-face with a moose perhaps only five feet away from the end of her nose. She just looked at him as if to say, "Yeah, right buddy, whatever. I've heard it all before."

Our flashlight beams hit the moose right in the eye, wiping out his night vision, and he stumbled into the cut of a small stream just beyond Jade, then clambered to his feet and ran around in circles.

I had bear spray, but didn't want to use it so we tried shouting.

"Hey, get the hell out of here!"

"You called him in here damnit, I think he's in love with my horse."

Now, the rest of the horse herd got into the act, galloping in with the awkward pogo-horse motion of hobbled horses to see what was up. They were more curious than anything. That did it. One nice mare on the end of a picket was one thing, but three more was too much for our moose. He turned and ran for the willows upstream, never to be seen again. We walked back to the fire, laughing and thankful that the mountain lady had kept it together.

The next fall, Jade had a repeat performance of her give-a-damn attitude. This time, Dave's older brother, Al, and I rode in a few days early to set up camp. We arrived as the sunlight angled across the golden fall grass in the meadow, home again, and feeling good. From the mountain to our south, way up over toward Wildcat Peak, we heard a bull elk bugle.

The camp rang with familiar sounds, the pounding of an axe head on a picket pin, the clink of hobbled horses feeding out in the meadow, the snap of pitch from the wall tent's woodstove. It was good to be back. Good to be home.

As we ate dinner back in the trees near the wall tent, we saw Jade's head suddenly come up. Jade served as the picket mare, the glue that keeps the herd together and calm. When she looks up, there will be something in the meadow, of that you can be sure.

We walked to the edge of the timber and looked in the direction she was looking. There, walking right through the horse herd, was a big boar grizzly, perhaps a hundred yards away. He sauntered across the meadow casually, stopping to sniff the air, digging a little bit at something, then moving on. Jade just watched him. The other horses watched her. It was a lesson I had learned a long time ago: the mountain lady keeps the calm picket mare balanced, centered. In the slanted sunlight, the grizzly bear's coat glowed cinnamon-gold and we watched, hardly breathing. After a while, he ambled out of sight, heading downstream, down the trail that we had ridden that morning. Jade bent her head back to the grass and again the sounds of quiet munching filled the air.

"That was something. Wow."

"Your heart beating yet?"

"Yep. Good thing the horses were cool with that big boy."

So it goes. That same week, Jade was offered two more chances to lose her mind, for it was a week of hard work. Dave and Al are hunting fools who go at it all day long, day after day. They don't often ride out of the mountains without meat.

Toward the end of the week, we each had taken a bull elk. The last one, a big bull that Dave shot on a distant shoulder of a faraway peak, took some doing to get out. At one point, after packing what seemed like the twentieth elk quarter off the mountain, I looked at Dave.

"Are we on vacation?"

"Oh yeah. How's your back?"

"Holding up, but we've got to stop killing things."

"Yeah, but you've still got to get a moose."

That year, I had finally gotten a license to hunt moose, but somehow, I'd spent the first half of the week concentrating on hunting and packing out elk. The next dawn, I was back on that same old worn-out and unmaintained trail that Jade had carried me down in the middle of the night. There was a big patch of dark timber that was full of moose signs and I stepped out of the saddle and started into the tall uncut.

I spent the day in that forest, walking slowly, listening. As the day faded, I finally saw a good bull moose bedded down in the black timber. I took a knee, and raised my rifle. It was full dark by the time Jade carried me back to camp.

The next morning, Al and I were back at the moose, cutting and sawing, doing a backwoods butcher job so we could get it all out. The animal was massive and awkward, but a few hours later we were ready to load.

Machina, The Machine, took the front quarters, tenderloin, and backstraps.

"Good God, these are the *front* quarters?"

"Yeah, they feel like elk hindquarters."

"How the hell are you going to eat all of this thing?"

"You're going to help me."

For some reason, the hindquarters, cape, and antlers went on Jade. It had been a long week and I wasn't thinking too clearly. Later, when I was down off that mountain, I weighed those hindquarters and they came in at 125 pounds each. With the cape and antlers at conservatively fifty pounds, Jade was carrying at least three hundred pounds. Pack horses should seldom carry more than 150 pounds and even now, I'm embarrassed that I overloaded my mountain gal so much and I tell myself that it wasn't much of a pack back to camp, only about three miles, but that is small consolation for my negligence.

I had shot the big bull on the edge of a dark bench. To the south, the bench ran out for twenty yards, and then the timber thinned and the mountain fell away steeply down to Pilgrim Creek and the trail. On the way up, we had plotted out a good route down off the mountain, one where we could switchback down the mountain, dropping perhaps five hundred feet before hitting the gentle main trail along the creek.

I threw a double-diamond hitch over the whole works on Jade, and cinched it down tight, or at least I thought I did. We mounted our saddle horses, and began the descent.

At first, everything went great. We moved slowly and I fell in behind Jade, who was being led behind Al's horse. As we made the first switchback, all was going fine.

"How's the load looking?" asked Al.

"Great. Top shelf."

We made the second switchback. Still no problems. It went like this until we made the final pitch down off the mountain. On one side was a steep ravine that we'd have to cross, and then a short climb up another bench to hit the trail. The tough part was over.

"Still looking good?"

"Fine and dandy."

Al's saddle horse dropped into the ravine, sliding on its forelegs down to the bottom, then climbing hard, neck arched into the bit, up the far side. Jade followed, the load rocking back and forth on her back, those big moose antlers sticking straight up in the air and swaying to and fro. The slide to the bottom went fine, but as Jade scrambled up the far side, the whole world came tumbling down.

"Holy crap! Al! Hey Al, stop!"

I had been looking down as my saddle horse did the slide into the ravine. I looked up just in time to see the whole load, all three hundred pounds of moose meat and antlers, go *voop!* right upside down. Now Jade had the weight down around her belly.

Time stood still and Jade turned her head slowly back and looked at me, as if to say, "You dumb bastards. What is next?"

I slid down off the saddle and hurried to get her tied up so we could repack. If ever a horse had an excuse to go insane and start kicking the hell out of the equipment and the pack, this was it, but Jade just stood there. We untied the hitch. The cinch, which was now across her withers, was so tight that I had to lift up on the dangling moose quarters while Al somehow got enough slack to unhitch the cinch and the whole works fell to the ground. Jade carefully stepped over the tangle of antlers, hide, meat, and pack-saddle and started grazing while we redid the whole thing all over again.

"Well, I'm getting enough practice packing on this trip," I said.

"No kidding."

"The next vacation I take, I'm going to go to Vegas and the heaviest thing I'm going to lift is a daiquiri."

We made it back to camp without any more mishaps, but that night, I made a mistake with Jade that I regret to this day.

Jade was our picket mare and picket horses are staked out on the best grass and the picket is moved many times. But you still feel sorry for them because all of their buddies have the freedom of grazing anywhere they want.

As we came into camp that night and after we had wrestled and wrenched that moose meat up onto the bear pole, we started hobbling all of the horses.

"Hey," I said. "You know these horses have been working hard. They aren't going anywhere. Let's just hobble the whole crew and I'll give Jade a break from the picket."

"Sounds like a plan."

We worked quickly to get hobbles on all of them and I left the halter on Jade for some reason. While I was working on one horse, I heard a crash and saw Jade struggling, with her halter somehow tangled into her hobbles, forcing her head down on her feet. She rested like that, her head far down between her front hooves, waiting for help, and I moved quickly and unsnapped the halter, thinking that had been a close call.

Only after she raised her head did I see the cut. A horse's head is covered by thin hide over thin bone. Their sinus cavities are laced like labyrinth caverns up from their nostrils to the brain. Somehow, Jade had rammed the sharpened end of a pine branch into her head between her eyes. An inch the other direction and she would have lost her right eye. I was sick. The cut was long and deep. She had hit that sharp pine branch hard enough to break into the nasal cavity and I was looking into her skull.

"This is a fine way to treat an animal who has busted her hump for us all day," I said.

Dave patted me on the shoulder. "Don't worry buddy, she'll be alright."

I was damned near bawling.

We doctored her as best we could, washing out the wound. She didn't act as if she were in pain and was more interested in eating, so we wrapped a bandage around her head, and turned her out with the rest of the herd. She looked as if she had been in a boxing match.

The next day, we rode out of the mountains and Jade acted her old self. That night, we dropped her off at the vet clinic and he did little more than we had already done. There was no way to stitch the thin skin, so she still bears that scar.

Jade is out in the pasture now, dozing in the warm spring sun, dreaming perhaps of the mountains, of trails to ride and streams to cross. Perhaps she's dreaming of those colts she has raised, those young, soft, playful creatures that are born with their mother's gait and their mother's attitude. Or maybe she is not dreaming at all, but is just enjoying the warm sun.

Two winters ago, Jade was pulled down thin, her withers prominent, the first slight bit of sway evident in her back. For the first time, I started to notice age in the mountain lady, the wrinkles at the corner of her mouth, the slow stretching in the morning. These days, she gets extra rations and special treatment. But there are still mountains to ride.

When you have a good horse, and are raising and training young ones, you seldom get a chance to ride a good, old horse. These Septembers, Jade has become Bob's horse. Bob is a retired forest ranger, father of Dave and Al, and he's been going on the hunts with us, to get back in the mountains with his boys, to read in the warm fall sun, to watch the horses, and tend camp while we are climbing mountains and hunting through big timber. Jade carries him in and carries him out and they've formed the shared bond of mountain veterans out in it.

Jade has taken care of old-timers and first-timers. She once carried a friend, who had torn his hamstring on an icy mountain slope, down a steep trail and safely back home. She got him home and she got me home. She deserves to doze out in the warmth of a western morning, to dream whatever dreams she dreams.

NINE

A Horse for Bill

—

Bill said he wanted to buy the next colt out of Jade and Ace. I said okay, but it would cost him because that was the only colt I was expecting. The previous year, the same combination of dam and sire had produced one hell of a colt, a big blaze-faced black beauty with twin hind socks and plenty of promise. A horse I called Grizz and a horse I was going to keep forever.

Bill laughed at that. He knew I was cash-poor and horse-rich. Or horse-poor.

"You can't keep them all, kid."

I allowed that that was true, but I could keep the good ones.

"Problem is, you've got too many good ones, kid. Sell the next one to me. Or sell me that yearling."

No, I'd keep Grizz.

"Well, we could trade something. What do you need? I got lots of stuff to trade."

Bill loves trading and I think he thinks he's the best trader in the valley. I knew he'd get to me if I let him because I was pretty sure he was right.

I told him I probably needed cash more than anything. When the time came, I'd sell him that next foal.

He pulled at his red suspenders and leaned back on the porch swing, looking across the morning up to the mountain. Off south, thin drifts of snow still clung to Flat Top, but I could see them going every day. They were big drifts. But from the front porch, those drifts looked as thin as fingernails and were getting smaller every day. I sipped coffee on that morning porch every day and those drifts way up there across the valley would be thinner, drawn down, melting at night. Even when the nights felt too cold and there was frost on the pastures in the morning, the drifts fell away. The snow would go and it would be planting time and there'd be another foal on the ground.

Bill took a loud sip from his coffee, cup cradled in a big hand, a work hand. It trembled a bit, a tiny splash of coffee staining his light-blue denim shirt, a drop pooling in the leather-tanned web of thin skin between thumb and forefinger. He didn't notice. A sideways look at me, sweat-yellowed Stetson pulled low against his brow, blue eyes squinting against the brightness. A spring sun. Even before seven it was getting too warm to be sitting around sipping something hot.

"I sure like that mare, and that stud, that's the gentlest stud I've ever seen. How'd you end up with two good horses like that, kid?"

A male meadowlark, full of himself, whistled from the buck and rail fence, so loud it made me jump. I shook my head and laughed.

Bill looked up toward the barn where Jade, thick with foal, stood and swished her tail at the first flies of the year. A gentle breeze out of the west wasn't enough to keep them away, but it was enough to carry the fragrance of sage from the bench above the barn, a scent mixing with the smell of the thaw, of mud and greening grass and sprouting cattails down in the coulee.

"You gonna get your garden in, kid? When the snow's off that mountain, you need to be planting. I want to buy the next colt out of that mare, kid. Well, I gotta get going." The man seldom sits still. "Let me know when that colt is on the ground, kid."

I told him I would.

He's a tall man, stooped a bit from the six foot, four inches of his prime. I've hardly ever seen him when he wasn't working. When those times come, he sips coffee and shows off pictures of big hook-jawed browns caught on his fishing trips to the Big Horn. Or he digs around in his basement and comes up with something he traded for. One year he went to Chile for the fishing and when he came back, he climbed the stairs from his basement with a sheepskin-covered, traditional Chilean saddle he twisted off of a *vaquero* for some worthless gee-gaw or another. But mostly he works and he doesn't slow down. I've driven by his place, meadows of green-purple alfalfa squeezed on three sides by houses, land too pretty and too close to town for its own good. He makes it work. He's out there when most are inside. Late. Running a tractor, or hunched over, attacking leafy spurge with a vengeance. Changing water. Moving stock from one pasture to another. He works and he likes to ride. He taught me to throw a diamond hitch years ago, demonstrating on a short pack mule tied inside one of his barns. The barn was full and fragrant with rich-green grass-alfalfa mix and a Bantam rooster crowed from a fence post. Bill grows the best hay in the valley. A calico cat rubbed against me as I watched Bill build the hitch. Talking. Calling me kid. Bill knows horses.

Foal watch. Rise every couple of hours. Go out to the barn, shine a light into that good mare's stall. Barn cat talking to you, ready for the day. Back to bed. Up again. A lady friend who is attending grad school back East is out for a visit and it's hard to pull myself out of bed every two hours. But I do it, leaving that warmth for the chill of a spring midnight. Without result. I've raised many colts and have yet to see one born. One day you wake up and there's a new horse standing out in the corral next to his mamma. It's that simple, that easy, that natural. All I did was lose sleep and a new horse was born when I wasn't there.

Jade is uncomfortably large, her bay hide taut over a huge belly, her bag swollen, and wax dripping from twin teats. She shifts her weight around, cocking one hind leg and then another. Any day now, any day. It has been exactly eleven months to the day since she was bred.

The blackbirds in the cattails down below the barn wake us at dawn on this May morning. Somewhere above the house, a snipe dances in the sky, the pitch of wind over his wings creating a sur-real, gurgling, almost-tropical sound. Now the whole world comes around, a pheasant crowing down on the neighbor's place, meadowlarks from every fence post.

It is a lazy morning, and we sit out on the porch and eat biscuits and gravy and sip coffee and watch the spring sun crawl across Flat Top, watch the wrinkles of the land flatten and then disappear as light takes over and shadows retreats. Jade stands with a hind leg cocked, three-legged again, tail going lazy in the warmth of the spring sun. We pour more coffee and kick back, rocking gently on the porch swing, listening to the ditch and its full complement of water. Making plans for the day, talking of our winters. Mine spent in the wilds of Wyoming, carrying a shotgun or a rifle or feeding horses and shoveling snow. Hers spent playing intramural volleyball, studying, going to ball games and concerts, good restaurants. Different worlds joined on a Wyoming spring morning.

An hour later, Jade is pacing the fence, swishing her tail. There aren't that many flies. She's uncomfortable. Foal watch goes from nothing to everything. Full swing.

"What's the vet's number?

"It's there on the fridge."

We watch from the porch. She is agitated, pacing in the corral. She kicks at her tight belly, swats that black long tail, spins in a circle, feet bunched tightly like a dog preparing its bed for the evening. Labor is on. Jade eases down into the middle of the corral, so fat with foal that she doesn't have far to drop. I grip the phone in one hand and we walk up to the barn cautiously. Even the dog knows something is up, for he stays close to my side rather than romping off into the cattails in search of that rooster pheasant.

Jade lies in the dirt for a while, moving only occasionally, and then only shifting a leg. She is sweating though and I can see tight muscles move, bunch, and relax. We watch and whisper. Heavy breaths now and the flexing of bay hide. Clear fluid pools at the base of her tail, pushed from inside and then followed by feet, miniature horse feet. Tiny feet no bigger than a child's fist. We wait and forget to breathe, then remember. Jade pushes and gains an inch more of the two feet, hooves down, a good sign. Jade pushes and embryonic fluid and a nose appears between those little feet. Another push and there's the head. Then shoulders. With a final, hard contraction, he plunges out of his mother, diving into a May morning. For a second, all is still and we forget to breathe again and flashes of doubt scatter through my brain. Stillborn? But then he lifts his head, the sack that was his home for eleven months tenting around him. I bend quickly and work the thin, strange wet bag off his head, his finely-sloped shoulders, his withers, and rump. Then I stand back, arm around my friend.

His hair is wet, dark, curly, and he seems all leg as he lies there on his chest and looks around at a new world. His mother eases up on her chest and bends her neck around to see what has come out of her. They touch noses and he makes a soft noise, almost catlike and she nickers, ever so soft.

"My God, Tom, that is beautiful."

A horse for Bill.

U

"Kid, you gotta come out and look at Joe. I put a tape on him. I think he's going to go over sixteen hands. How big is that stud?"

"He's sixteen."

"And that mare's a little mare. I don't want him to get too big. It gets harder and harder to get on them. But come out here, I want you to see this."

Joe is no longer the baby colt that I picked up after his mother got acquainted with him, that I worked to imprint and get used to human hands, to dogs and cats and ladies from grad schools back East. Now he is a big sorrel horse, marked only with a single star and he's about as tame as a lapdog. Even at three when most horses are awash in adolescent nonsense, this horse acts like a completely finished veteran.

"I sent him to the trainer and they had a couple of boys riding him in a few days. Told them I wanted to have him broke so an old man wouldn't have any trouble. They were roping off of him in two days."

Bill swings up on Joe in one fluid motion. The horse's size, so far, doesn't seem to matter much. Bill is grinning.

"Okay, now watch this."

The horse crosses a narrow wooden bridge over Squaw Creek.

"Okay, now watch this."

The horse backs up four or five steps at Bill's asking.

It goes on like this, one command given, one perfect response. I'm beginning to think that Bill got to me a bit when we agreed on a price. Bill demonstrates as Joe foxtrots around the pasture, reining perfectly, acting sensible, crossing the wooden bridge over Squaw Creek again as if he'd done it a thousand times.

"I just hope he doesn't get any bigger, kid."

"This darned horse won't stop growing, kid."

Another year has passed.

"He's an honest seventeen hands. Come out to the house and take a look at him. Take a look at the pictures of our trip too."

Bill has just returned from New Mexico, where he and his girlfriend and son and granddaughter had ridden a section of the Continental Divide Trail from Antelope Wells to north of Grants.

"Come on out to the house, I want to show you some pictures from our trip."

They had touched the border of Mexico, and then started north through the mesquite flats of New Mexico's Bootheel, trailing a couple of good walking mules, with Bill riding Joe. Two members of the party leapfrogged ahead with a pickup and horse trailer and set up camp somewhere along the route, while two rode the trail. They slept on the ground under the clear New Mexico spring skies and swapped off between riding and staging for the next day.

"We're going to do that every year until we've ridden to Canada."

The horse is indeed an honest seventeen hands, too big for most men, but Bill is a tall man. Joe is dog-gentle, straight, and well-gaited, a true mountain horse. We walk around him and he munches treats from Bill's hand.

"Hey kid, I hear that mare's pregnant again. If it's a horse colt I'd like to buy him. I'd like to have a matched set of these horses."

I laugh and tell him okay and think that someday I'd like to be eighty years old buying a weanling colt and riding from Mexico to Canada on a horse that knows how to walk.

TEN

Selling Out

—

John needed a new horse. He didn't want one. He wanted the one
he had, but she was done. Two summers ago, in a strange pasture,
his fine, gentle bay mare Hannah had met her end. Somehow, on
something, she had cut herself to the bone on the right front, a cut
deep, ugly, and permanent. John was out of town, in Washington
D.C. on business, and how long the good mare stood there bleeding is something he didn't want to think about. There was enough
blood, it seemed, for two horses and when the neighbors found

her, head down, three-legged, they called the first vet they could find. Time didn't matter though. Location was everything. Had the wound been a half-inch higher, she might have made it to ride another mountain trail, but it wasn't. It hit the coronary band, the ring of tissue from which the horse hoof grows. It is like the bed of a fingernail. The band was severed.

John spent money on her. She was a pet, the kind of horse that you could turn loose on your lawn to graze while you drank a beer on a summer evening. She'd eat her fill, then come hang her head over your shoulder and keep you company. I had raised her as a colt, my first colt, cradled her in my arms, encouraged her to nurse from mother Jade. When things went south in my marriage, I sold Hannah to pay some bills and she found her way down to Colorado. Later, when I was flush with cash, I tracked down the man who owned her, and I bought her back. She was in my mare herd for a time and I raised one good colt from her. Then John needed a good one and I knew that he was the kind of person who would form a partnership with her, a long one. The kind of person who you would want to care for your first colt. She was marked like her mother, that unusual blaze-faced bay. And she had a heart like her mother's. She was a mountain horse. But now she was done.

The hoof never grew right. The severed band caused a flaw and as the hoof grew, it always had a crack in it. Right down the middle. Perhaps that caused the limp. Early on, she moved as if she were in hobbles. Hopping, slinging her head, lunging forward. As the months wore on, the limp got better and we began to hope, a little bit. But there was still a limp. Even a person with an untrained eye could see that. A limp enough to keep her out of the mountains. Through two years and multiple surgeries, she just never was sound again. She had ridden the toughest of mountain trails and she was the kind of camp horse that you could leave unhobbled out there in the tall meadow grass. But she wouldn't ever go there again. Couldn't. One summer evening, John sat on his porch and watched the nighthawks dive over his place. She was out there with her pasture companion, Topper. She could bear some weight on the leg. She could raise fine babies, but there would be no riding her and John knew it. He had known it, but he didn't want to admit it. He never did find out what she had cut herself on and it took a long time for him to forgive himself for putting her out in that strange pasture. He had wanted to rest his own grass, to let it grow by letting the horses eat from another pasture, but the price had been far too high. A month's worth of grass had cost him dearly. Now he needed another horse.

"You know anybody with a good one?"

I said I'd ask around, thinking about Montana, and my friend Curt. Up there, just outside Red Lodge, Curt raised some good horses. Topper had come out of Montana. So did a couple of other horses I knew. All good ones. For several years, Curt and I did a mare swap with me delivering one or two mares to his stallion and Curt sending a couple of mares my way. We'd rendezvous at the fairgrounds in Meeteetse, exchanging long looks at our breeding stock, soaking in the warm spring sun, catching up on the winter's doings. Curt always had good stuff, clean and gentle with good straight legs. I made the phone call.

Curt's wife Lou answered and we caught up and then I asked about Curt.

"Let me put him on."

He had come up through the ranks in the Forest Service and he was known as a good man who rode a good horse. The last duty had been as a supervisor in the national forest outside Billings. He knew horses and he wanted a home where he could raise a few. When a few hundred acres came up for sale while he was still on the job, he jumped at it. The place sat up against a hill, with a long view across a valley and whitetail deer in the river bottoms. He had one good stud with lines right back to the foundation of the breed, and then as things grew, he bought another one, a flashy young palomino that could gait in its sleep. He retired and bought more stock. Twenty or more mares. There was enough work around the place that he hired a woman and her son to do the horse breaking and he kept a steady progression of young horses going through. He always had one or two, maybe three, for sale. The last time I saw him, his operation was growing and you could feel the excitement in his voice. He was raising good horses and each colt on the ground was something he invented, something he and Lou created. A horse. That's something. Word was getting out and people called him cold, asking after horses they'd never seen, calling on reputation alone. A horse breeder works years for that kind of word.

I told him what I was looking for, a young horse with some potential. Didn't need to be ready to ride, John could handle breaking it. Preferably a gelding.

"Come up. I've got a couple that fit that bill. I'm selling out."

I crooked the phone against my shoulder, not saying anything. Selling out. Curt was selling out. He had bought the young stud only a year ago. It didn't make sense, but I didn't ask. I didn't want to know the answer. Selling out.

We drove north in the last heat of August, up out of Cheyenne, across the prairie, grasshoppers slapping against the windshield. John's Ford rumbled along, easily pulling the empty horse trailer, eight hours of blacktop ahead of us. Listening to the local country music station until we ran out of range, then tuning into another station, losing it, tuning in to something else. The Laramie

Mountains stood on our left, huge black cumulous clouds building on the west. The prairie stretched east and north forever, tan in the late-summer heat, baked, done.

We talked of horses and our hunt now less than a month away and we scratched our heads through logistics, thinking about the trail ahead, and counting up hunters and horses and potential elk packed out. Would we have enough stock for all the hunters? If we got a good colt from Curt, that was possible.

At Casper, we pulled into a truck stop and fueled up. We watched the people swing through the place, past the aisles of CB radios and fuzzy dice, past the colorful bags of chips and rows of pop. They stood robotic in line, expressionless. The cashier, too, had the same look: as if the world was something to be suffered stoically and without interest. I wondered if the road had given us a similar patina.

We headed north, back on the interstate, Casper fading in the rearview mirror, nothing but sagebrush prairie and oil rigs ahead. The sun splashed the land with its last rays and for once, there was no wind on the plains. By the time we reached Buffalo, it was fully dark and we were tired, but we turned west, up the highway, climbing into the Bighorns, rolling past roadside deer, climbing higher. A few miles out of town, rain splashed on the windshield, soft at first, and then picking up to thrum loudly on the cab of the truck, drowning out the sound of the diesel and the latest country station. It came hard enough to wash the grasshopper juice off the windshield and the road blurred in front of us as we climbed the mountain in the dark.

We turned off the highway where a forest service sign pointed toward a campground. John ground the truck into second and pulled off on a high ridge, shy of the campground and other people. The dogs were anxious to get out and galloped off into the rain while we took a look around for a place to roll out our sleeping bags. I wrapped mine in a heavy tarp, threw it under the truck and crawled in. The rain had slacked and it was relatively dry underneath, dry enough anyway.

At dawn we rose rumpled and tired. We moved quickly, throwing our bags into the pickup, and climbing in. It was fading summer and there was a crispness to the air, a wet coldness that foretold of an autumn to come. It smelled that washed-clean smell, but there was a chill to it, the kind of temperature that makes you think you are sticking your head in a freezer on a hot summer's day.

We drove for a while in the dawn light of the mountain, not saying anything, fuzzy from lack of caffeine, watching the sun wash slowly across the mountain, drying the meadow dew, throwing warmth onto the land, turning the lodgepole pine forests a glowing yellow-green. At the base of the mountain, we stopped for weak coffee and then motored on, out across the Bighorn Basin, all clay and greasewood sprawled before us. As we headed toward Cody, we saw herds of feral horses on a ridgeline, paints and roans shining bright in the morning light, heads down. Young colts and mares and perhaps a stallion there, its head up, watching the land and the highway and a Ford diesel and horse trailer rattling by.

We get to Curt and Lou's place in the late morning and the ranch dogs welcome us as we step out into the yard, stretching tired road muscles, moving slowly and stiffly. Lou greets us first, a quick quiet smile, a fit woman in her fifties, wearing jeans.

"I'll go get Curt," she says, and she leaves us there standing in the dust, leaning over the fence railing, looking at a pen full of year-lings. A buckskin or two, a young bay that moves nicely.

Curt comes around the corner of the house and his grip is strong. He says hello with a smile and he listens to our tale of the trip up from Wyoming. He moves easily across the ranch yard and talks about his old stud with a smile, pointing out the young horses out of him, then the excitement in his voice building as he points out the stock out of his new stud. Both of the buckskins came from the new yellow horse.

"I really like the way they are put together."

I agree with him and John asks him about geldings.

"I've got a couple. A nice bay that's three that you need to see. I might have a buyer for him."

From another horse trader, I might think that was a line, a lure thrown out there to entice a quick sale, a chip laid down for bargaining: Buy this one quick because someone else wants him. But with Curt, I know this is the truth. If he says there's another buyer, there's another buyer. John seems to sense that this is an honest man as well.

Curt's help arrives, another fit ranch woman and her son. The boy deftly saddles the good-looking bay and takes him for a spin around the pasture. The horse moves well and the training shows. He's gentle and together. John looks on appreciatively and then Curt mentions a young palomino, this one out of his old stud and he gestures toward another pen where a trim yellow horse is nuzzling the back of his pasture mate, a fine paint.

There is something about buying a new horse that perks up one's soul. Potential in a young horse is like a flower that has yet to blossom. This horse, you think, might make the best horse you've ever owned. It is thoughts like this that keep you in the buying business, and if you are in the selling business, it is an addiction leading to more horses bought than sold. The young palomino is like that, for you can see in his form a young horse with a heart and you can see, if you tilt your head just right and squint a bit, a

filled-out, solid mountain horse. The boy walks the palomino gelding around a bit, showing off the two-year-old and when John says
he'll take him, Curt smiles.

"That's fine. That's real fine."

My friends talk price and it is reasonable and money is
exchanged. Curt smiles again and then he asks me if I know of
other people who might want good horses for the mountains.

"I want to find them all good homes."

"Well, I'll keep it in mind." I do not ask.

John and I stand there in the rising heat of the day, uncomfortable in the silence. It has been that kind of morning, since there
have been words floating in the air, talk of horses and potential and
of mountains and rides. But there has been the unsaid. And the
unasked. I do not know why Curt is selling everything, selling his
dream. I'm not sure I want to hear the answer.

Now even the birds seem to be silent and I find myself wondering why we humans always seem to feel the need to fill space
with noise, instead of just listening to nothing. Too quiet. This
moment stretches for a time and I am lost in it, soon forgetting
that I was uncomfortable. Instead I just watch the horses in the
corral flick their tails at lazy flies, dozing in the warm sun. All
three of us stand like this. Quiet. Then the words come from Curt.

They are soft words, told slowly, and there is no pain in them. Only acceptance, but there is a tint of worry there too.

"I've been diagnosed with liver cancer."

Words don't come. They can't come.

"The doctor says I have about two months. I'm ready. But I need to unload these horses. Some are going to good homes and Lou can keep Top Hand around and a few others."

I say something lame about thinking of other people who might want a good horse, but those words offer little comfort.

Curt smiles at this. "Tom, I do want to show you this filly I've got. She's something special."

"Okay."

She is a year old and her frame is one of perfect proportions. Some colts are like this, as if they are born in the dimensions of their life and it's all a matter of scale. The colt will grow and mature and become a horse, but the dimensions, the proportions, will not change. She is already a horse in miniature. Others are like the gangly two-year-old that John just paid for. They grow awkwardly and then, sometime in their fourth or sixth year, you wake up and find out you have a horse that is put together well. But this one is perfect and I can see why Curt is proud of her. She was born on the fifth of May and her name is Cinco de Mayo.

She glimmers in the morning sun, a palomino with a hide as blonde as autumn grass, that shimmering white-yellow of wheat stubble. Or a sun-bleached surfer girl's mane. I watch her for a while and then Lou brings up a halter and we work it over her young nose. She is gentle, like all the young stock in Curt's pens and she moves out well under the lead. I like how she moves, how her hind hooves stretch over the track of the fronts, and how her head is level and put on right.

"I like that little filly, Curt. I can see why you are proud of her."

I say these words as one horse breeder to another, a compliment. I do not need another horse. I have only a little pasture and not enough grass for the horses I already have. For once, I have trimmed down my herd to match the land that I have and that is a rare thing for a person who loves living with horses. I am telling myself this, but all the while, there's a nagging inside that says perhaps I could slip her in somehow. And, I could help a friend and helping a friend is one of life's greatest rewards.

John looks over at me. "We're hauling back a three-horse trailer with one horse in it."

The man has a way of stating the obvious.

I purposely left my checkbook at home, thinking about addictions and afflictions. It's a practice that has never worked, despite my best intentions. I look over at him and he smiles and gestures with his head to join him.

"Give me a minute, Curt."

We walk to the corral railing and lean up against it, looking off toward the mountains. I feel the rough wood against my forearms and the sun on my back. Everything seems to have more texture, more life. I vow to appreciate the little things like sun on your shirt and the smell of horses in a corral.

"I didn't bring my checkbook."

"I did."

"Well, I'm good for it."

"You can pay me when you get back home."

I turn back toward Curt, who is sitting in a lawn chair under the wide spread of a cottonwood, looking out across the place that he built, out at the horses that he created and raised. I can see that he's drawn and a little pale and it is either worry or pain that etches his face. He's a deeply religious man and he finds comfort there.

"I'll take that filly, Curt."

I can see the relief washing over the man, a quiet smile, a relaxation that seems to ease the tension in his posture.

"That's real fine. Real fine."

John writes out another check and now we have two Montana palominos to take back to Wyoming.

"Come on into the house and we'll have some coffee."

We sit in the kitchen and drink coffee and listen to the afternoon wind rustling the cottonwood leaves outside and Curt talks. He talks of the horses he's raised and smiles when he thinks of some of the places he's ridden.

Then he talks about his time.

"I'm ready," he says. "I just worry about Lou."

She ducks her head and stares at her coffee cup, and smiles a sad smile. She slips a hand over and cradles his in hers for a brief moment, a tender brush between husband and wife.

He talks about grudges and forgiveness. I am reminded of Mitch Albom's book *Tuesdays with Morrie*, a sad yet uplifting tale of an old man with a great attitude, who is dying of Lou Gehrig's disease, yet has a chance to talk about his life and living before he goes. "Forgive yourself before you die," the old man says. "Then forgive others."

Curt's words are similar and I am caught up in wondering how many of us spend valuable time holding a grudge, or feeling sad or bitter when the world has more to offer. "Don't hold bitter feelings," he says. "It will just eat you up. You only get so much time and you shouldn't spend it feeling anger toward something or someone."

We absorb these words in silence, sipping coffee, listening to the kitchen clock tick on the wall.

An hour later we load the two palominos into the horse trailer and they load easily, for Curt and his helpers have been working with them since they hit the ground as youngsters.

We stand in the ranch yard for a while, letting the horses get used to the trailer, standing there and not saying anything. I shake Curt's hand, look him in the eye, and I think about those rendezvous in Meeteetse, about meeting Curt and Lou and exchanging horses and thinking of the kinds of colts we'd raise. How his stallion throws a better hip and rump on colts than mine, but how mine throws great legs and nice heads and how this partnership between him and me has produced some fine horses for mountain trails. I shake his hand again and try not to think that it will be the last time.

"It's been a pleasure, Curt."

"Thank you."

We drive south toward the toe of the Absarokas, toward the town of Red Lodge. The mountains rise off south and west and go forever, a shadowing hulk of a range that stretches all the way to Yellowstone. We do not play the radio, instead just listening to the rumble of the road and the diesel, and feeling the sway of two Montana blondes in the horse trailer, headed to a new home.

It is a long time before either one of us speaks.

ELEVEN

Letter to Lucy Gray

—

I don't even know what a godfather does. I have a vague idea and I think there may be presents involved. I could ask around, get some thoughts on what other people think it should be, but I kind of like having a blank canvas to make it up as we go along.

Your Dad came up to Montana this summer to ride and camp with me and that's when he asked me if I'd be your godfather. He said he and your Mom had talked it over and it seemed right. I laughed it off, but I also have got to tell you, it brought tears to my eyes. The honor of it. We were heading up into the West Pioneers on a four-day horsepacking trip, your Dad riding my old mare, Mac, me on Black Jack, and my new young filly, Sis, carrying our food and a bottle of good Irish whisky. We got rained on, caught some fish, shared that bottle, and had lots of good laughs. In the mornings, when it was quiet and we fed twigs into old coals and watched flames rise in the campfire, I thought about what it means to be a godfather. To have someone I'm going to watch grow up and become a young woman.

This morning, your morning, I hiked out to my upper pasture, caught old Mac and rode her bareback to the house. I didn't know you had been born, but already in my head, I was thinking about what I might say to you. What I might teach you. Is there something an old bachelor can teach a little girl? Some lesson? Some way of going? What do I know of raising children with no experience of my own?

It's horseshoe time again. Hunting season is on me and there's a wind off the Tobacco Roots pushing leaves off the cottonwoods, telling me it's here, and so I caught Mac and let Jack and Sis run loose, bringing them down to the barn to meet the farrier. In the stirred-up wind, the horses skittered. I swung up on old Mac with just a halter, and she pranced and threatened to run with the other two and I thought to myself, *I'm getting too old for this crap*. As the other two galloped off in the loose wind, I worried that I might find myself on top of my head, but pride kept me up there even though she jigged and jogged and threatened to tip me off. She defies her age and I'm at the age when I deny mine.

When I got back to the house, there was a message from your Dad that you had been born. And so you are here, Lucy Gray. A new soul in a complicated world. I'm a new godfather in that same world. And here are my first words to you: get outside, find the passion in your life, love someone, and throw yourself at it.

There's a solace in nature that you'll find just by putting yourself there. I know your parents will take you into the mountains and desert and open plains and you'll find that peace. You will learn to ski and ride a bike and a horse. You'll learn to row a boat down a beautiful river, cast a fly to a rising trout, eat wild raspberries right off the stem.

It's a wonderful life, this life spent outside. When life is troubling you, go there. Learn the wildflowers, know the birds, the insects. Listen. Grow a garden. Eat farm eggs and elk steak. We live life in a world of machines, but our true nature is nature. This is where our species has evolved, in a world that is dangerous and exciting, a world beyond our inventions. Breathe in that clean air. Get outside.

There will come a time in your life when it will seem as if stress is all you are swimming in. It is at this moment that you will need to open the door and step out into it. Away from the indoor pressures into a space big enough to wash it all away. Get on a horse. Put on some hiking boots. Pick up a fly rod. Get away. Get out.

I've been lucky in my life, for my passion is the outdoors, and the outdoors is my work. But there are many other passions. Find yours. Most of all, have fun. We only get one of these things called life. It's not a dress rehearsal. Find something that you love to do and do it often. Find something worth fighting for and fight for it. Stand up for people and creatures that can't stand up for themselves. Argue for your beliefs, but be civil about it. Try to see both sides, for that way you'll be able to understand others and your convictions will be all the more firm for that understanding. But more than anything, have fun. Enjoy it.

Your life is going to be filled with many great people, people you'll love deeply and without condition. Good people, starting with your parents and spreading out from there. You are born into goodness, with rich souls all around you. You'll meet many and you'll know, by looking into their eyes, the depth of their goodness. Love them. Love animals the same way and watch how others treat their fellows and how they treat animals. You can do a lot of weeding if your own eyes are open.

Finally, go at it hard. If the road is rocky, take it. If it's tough and difficult, it's worth doing. If it were easy, anybody could do it. No man has made a good name for himself by taking the easy way out. No matter how much it sucks, suck it up.

And so there it is. Get outside, be passionate about it, love well, and work hard.

And always remember, if you need help in this world, if you need someone to protect you and love you and help you fight the fight, he lives in Montana and runs a string of great bird dogs and rides cranky old mares bareback.

Welcome to the world, Lucy Gray.

TWELVE

A Mountain

—

"You have any idea what time it is?"

John squints at the sun, fading toward the western horizon, dropping down toward the Yellowstone Plateau.

"Oh, I'd guess about one or so. What do you think?"

"That sounds about right."

Neither one of us has remembered to wear a watch. Somehow, in the predawn darkness, we both rose from our sleeping bags, pulled down a cup of coffee, and started to hike without remembering. The quick routine of getting going, getting out there, pushed us. An urgency. Lunch had been packed the night before and our packs carried gear for the mountain: a spotting scope, binoculars, survival and first aid kits, maps.

It was the mountain before us that drew my own thoughts, a ridge covered in alpine fir. The day before, we had glassed some sheep up beyond that mountain of fir, up high in a timberline bowl where they could look across the massive Trident Plateau, all the way to Yellowstone and see any trouble coming. There were rams in the bunch and we wanted to get up there, up in the tall country where we could stalk and perhaps find a good one. A decent ram.

This morning, John and I had climbed up an avalanche chute on the mountain of fir, then crested a long ridge and walked out into timberline. We climbed more, breathing hard and stopping, but always up. In a basin that had been hidden from our binoculars the day before, we found a band of ewes and lambs. By then the sun was high enough that it felt like noon, or at least our stomachs told us it was time to fuel up. We sat with our backs against lichen-etched boulders and watched the band of wild sheep and we glassed other ridges. After a time, we rose and pushed on. Up some more. We were on a massive plateau that stretched east to west in the Teton Wilderness, a plateau that dropped off on its western rim into Yellowstone National Park. It was some of the most remote and wild space left in this country and it seemed as if it belonged just to us.

As the sun tilted west, we talked about circling back to camp, about dropping and losing all of that elevation that we gained. It was only the second day of the hunt and we planned on two hard weeks in these mountains hunting both sheep and elk. There will be another day, but there is always another ridge to peek over as well. Off to my right, to the west, was another basin and I told John to stay put while I scouted it. I walked off, carrying my spotting scope, pack, and rifle.

In that mountain bowl, with a view of all the world, were three good rams. I laid there for a while and looked at them. They were bedded and dozing in the warmth of the September sun. I looked hard at the largest of the rams and made a decision, sliding my rifle up onto my pack and easing my thumb up onto the safety.

Now, with the sun as our timepiece, there is a dead ram at my feet.

We kick it around a while and John decides to go for three horses. Two to ride, one to pack. I watch him ease his way down the steep slope, working over tricky footing until he hits the timberline and disappears into the trees. I am alone now, except for the ram and the mountain under me and the view west.

The life of the hunter is one of conflict. For every mountain, there is a valley. With the ease of pulling the trigger comes the hard work of making what was once a magnificent animal into meat. With the anticipation of the hunt, the dreaming, and the planning, comes the reality of logistics and the hard work of getting there and getting it done. And, if you have lived right and done well, you will also feel the battling emotions of joy and sorrow when that animal lies dead at your feet.

I sit there for a long time, or what seems like a long time. I take one glance at his bright eyes staring straight up at the Wyoming sky, the same sky that I have harnessed my soul and life to, and sit down where I do not have to look at him. The grass is still green here and among the scree and tufts of green grow alpine forget-me-nots. The scent of some other flower fills the air. There is a light breeze from the west and the sun is warm on my face. I look at the view, his last view. Mountain Creek sweeps away below me, away west into the park. Turret Peak and Table Mountain rise off in the distance, way off down in Yellowstone, cloaked in haze from some distant September fire off in Idaho. I can see the big meadow where we had camped in August during a scouting trip and no doubt glassed this very same ram. It is one hell of a view.

I try to thank somebody for this great gift of a life. Somebody, something, but it seems pretty hollow and false, somehow. Then I bend to the knife work, the drudgery of cutting an animal that has just been alive into pieces. I think about the winters up here, harsh and windswept, and somehow he had survived it. He had lived up there above the trees for seven long years, enjoying the gentle summers and basking in the warm light of autumn and welcoming the melt of spring.

When his friends—two lesser rams that I had passed up in favor of his more massive horns—come back and stand around watching me, I certainly do not feel any better. I apologize to them and it still feels hollow. After I am done, I look over at him.

I sit there in those thoughts and in that west-dropping sunlight and I wait. I do not know how long, but then I hear the tinkle of loose rock on horse hoof and John is leading a young mare up through the rocks. It is a steep slope, tough on a horse, especially a young one, but she scrambles and drops to her knees once, and comes up. I watch them come up from the timberline, where the whitebark pine gives up. It seems like a long way down there, and I think about how much time I would have to escape if I were a bighorn sheep. Unless the danger comes from above—as I did with this good ram—this is the safest place in the world.

When John gets to me he tells me the bad news.

"I think it was more like four than one. It's getting pretty late."

I could feel it too and there are clouds rolling in from the west.

We work quickly, tying the quarters and the ram's head and cape on the young mare, then carefully leading her down out of there. She slips and slides, her back feet braced up under her belly, her front legs stiff on the downhill, slithering down over slide rock and slick grass. Occasionally, she has to jump down from one short rock ledge to another. This, I think, is no way to treat a horse. Let alone a horse that I have raised, that I have lifted in my arms when she was a baby, who I have curried and clucked to. We do not drop straight down, for the angle is too steep, but the zigzag is also tough and the pack threatens to slip even though it is well-balanced. Even the best-thrown pack would threaten to slip on this slope.

By the time we reach the saddle horses, the clouds have rolled over the sun and it is nearly dusk. It feels good to be there though, at the head of a long ravine. Ahead of us lie several miles of deep timber, most of it burnt up in the fires of 1988, the same fires that charred Yellowstone and the same fires that made this some of the finest game country in the world. Where the saddle horses are tied to the gray skin of the whitebark pines it is relatively flat and we both swing up and start riding toward camp. One of the horses,

Jade, the mother of the young colt we packed, has an uncanny knack of knowing the woods and the way home. We let her lead.

It gets dark quickly and in the burned timber, I tuck my head down, and try to keep from being strained right out of the saddle by some unseen limb. We stagger like this for a while, with the mountain mare carefully picking her way, but soon it is full-on dark and we are not making much progress. We are both taking a steady beating from unseen tree branches and it is getting old fast.

The decision comes easily for both of us. We have enough between us so we can spend the night out if we have to and when we come to a big Englemann spruce that somehow escaped the burn, we agree. We will stop here and wait out the night.

As we work the sheep up into another tree and tie off the horses, it starts to sprinkle. By the time we get a fire going under the protective limbs of the big tree, it is raining hard, but we are tucked back in there and relatively dry. I offer John half a can of smoked oysters that I keep in my saddle bags for just such a situation but he turns me down. The can has been in there for a year, but they taste pretty good.

It drizzles all night. We sleep on either side of the fire and one of us stokes the coals all during the night. The horses are quiet and I try not to think about grizzlies in the thick timber. I think about sheep and about the logistics of getting that bighorn sheep out.

At dawn, we are both up and moving surprisingly quickly despite our lack of caffeine. I mount the mountain mare and grab the lead rope attached to her daughter, and we head off down the mountain. Now, in the full light, it is a relatively easy ride and all we have to do is get to camp. In two hours, we are there, and our camp companions walk from the tent with mugs of hot coffee. They were expecting us, not worried. A night out in tough country is nothing unusual. But it is good to be home.

THIRTEEN

A Machine

—

We are thirty-five miles from the trailhead. There are five of us, all with elk tags and the rest of the next week could be spent elk hunting. We talk it over as we eat breakfast, then I make a decision. I will ride for the road, packing out the sheep. I will take the meat to the butcher and the head to the taxidermist, then I will come back in and hunt elk for a week. I will try to do this in-and-out expedition in three days: a day out, a day in town, a day back in. There are two horses in camp that can make that kind of ride, a good bay gelding to do the packing and the gray mare. The gray mare is otherworldly. Her registered name is something silly like Lady's Fancy Sensation, but we call her Machina. Spanish for "machine." Secretly, I call her the Hell Bitch, after the gray mare ridden by Tommy Lee Jones's character, Woodrow F. Call, in *Lonesome Dove.*

The way a sewing machine works. She moves like this. Fluid. Smooth, fast. You can kick her into a higher gear by just relaxing on the reins a bit. There is no putting a heel to this horse. You find yourself pulling back on her. All day long.

She moves automatically and seemingly without effort. I've never ridden a horse that moves like this. When I purchased her as a nine-year-old, her papers had the signatures of four other owners, a sure warning sign that here was a horse that had issues. I soon found out what those issues were: she moved too fast for most riders to keep up, even riders on the fastest mountain horses. Here was a horse that would not thrive in a pack string. But leading one good-moving pack horse over tough terrain for thirty-five miles? This was the horse I would want to be on more than any other, even more than my brown-eyed girl, Jade.

At dawn the next day, I mount Mac and turn in the saddle. The others have their rifles slung and are heading off in different directions after elk. They wave at me and I turn the mare to the trail.

We cover ground at a fast walk and the pack horse follows easily, the lead rope slack in my hand. He moves well, the only pack horse that could keep up with Mac. We click down the Mountain Creek trail and the outfitter's camp. A guide is heading out with two dudes and they stop in the trail and talk to me, admiring the sheep. The grey mare dances sideways while I talk, her neck arched, her temper flaring because she has to stand there while I talk. She side-passes one way and the other and then I apologize to the hunters and turn to the trail.

"Sorry, this damned horse wants to go."

Words she has likely heard many times before. Especially "this damned horse."

So we do. The trail winds through burnt timber and green forest, down a slope where in August we had seen a good-sized grizzly among the fireweed, down into the park, across a creek, and then climbing toward Eagle Pass. The mare never slows, never breathes hard. A sewing machine. Or a clock. Or any kind of machine. My heart beats hard with the excitement of a ride like this and then we are over Eagle Pass, and down through black timber, and then out into Eagle Creek Meadows, then splashing through Eagle Creek, and following the lava rimrock above its little canyon. By late afternoon, I am splashing through the North Fork of the Shoshone River and have unloaded the bay pack horse and have both horses in the trailer. Only big old Lad in his prime could keep up such a pace and I never owned him in his prime.

Night finds me home and in the morning, I throw hay and grain to the bay and the gray and I thank them for the good ride. The bay gelding kept up well, but he looks tired. The Machine, though, paces in the corral and has her ears forward. She wants to go again. I take the sheep to the taxidermist, who admires the curve of his horns, the job I did with his cape. I am awash in the same emotions that caught me on the mountain, thinking strange things about how a wilderness sheep that rarely even heard the sounds of overhead jet airplanes is now hearing the sounds of humans and of traffic and town.

The meat goes to the butcher, and I load the horses into the horse trailer and head back to the trailhead. At dusk, I am there and I find two of our party. They are heading out, discouraged by the amount of elk signs in the mountains, tired with the hunting.

Well, I'm going in anyway. John and his brother, Dave, are still in there, waiting for me to return. I crawl up into the nose of the trailer and snuggle deep into my sleeping bag.

At dawn, I am on Machina again and I am heading up the trail, her pace in as fast as it was going out. Some horses are one-way animals, moving quickly when headed out toward home, and going slow in. The mare is not like this at all. She wants to go and she has her neck arched into it. If I relax the reins just a bit, she would move up into a canter and lope all the way back into camp. I keep her at a fast foxtrot and the bay pack horse, now carrying nothing but the sawbuck pack saddle, keeps up.

We reverse everything, dropping down off Eagle Pass, riding through the park, and then hitting the wilderness boundary on the west, all the way to Mountain Creek. The mare clicks right along, *tick, tick, tick*. It is as automatic as some kind of assembly line machine. We see more hunters and stop and talk for a bit, but she dances sideways again and I curse her. It is a love-hate thing. She never stops.

By afternoon, I arrive at camp and find my friends John and Dave sitting there and camp torn down. They report that there has been enough hunting pressure to spook the elk back into the park and they would like to go try another hunt area on the other side of the range with what is left of their vacation. They want to leave in the morning. The next morning. Another thirty-five miles right back out. I shrug at this.

At dawn, we rise and pack the string. The gray mare, the Machine, stands with her ears up. There are thirty-five miles ahead of us. If I am to ride them again, I will ride them astride the Machine.

FOURTEEN

The Horse

—

When I bestride him, I soar, I am a hawk. He trots the air, the earth

sings when he touches it.

—Henry V, *3.7, William Shakespeare*

The way the high country light from a going-away-day bounced off his hide. I remember. Montana timberline and the horses grazing out in a tall meadow, tails swishing at mosquitoes. Stringing up a fly rod for a few casts, dinner done, but light still out there on meadow and on stream where it bent through it. Light on him. He anchored the herd, dominant. They wouldn't leave without him.

We rode that week on trails that had seen only a smattering of human tracks all summer long. We rode through stands of lodgepole and whitebark, up into tall country that peeled off into the drainages of ocean birthwater. There, up there, up high, it was a melding of man and horse and wilderness.

You could say I invented him. His father had been the tall black stud, a refined big son of a gun who could travel backcountry trails with speed and precision, who would leave lesser horses panting and sweated and spent. You'd be fishing by the time those poorer mounts arrived streamside.

I named his mother Jade. It seemed appropriate, considering Wyoming, considering the horse. Smooth and silky. Smart. She had a homing instinct like no horse I'd seen, before or since. Elk-country blizzard, back-side-of-the-moon dark, all of those. Tough conditions when you couldn't see the palm in front of your face and yet she walked true and pure and without misstep. She got you home.

And so he was born. I called him Grizz. It seemed like a fitting name, considering Wyoming, considering where I hunted elk. At birth he was as tawny as an antelope fawn, with a big, wide blaze and hind stockings that went up over the hocks. And he was something. From the very beginning, he was special. Of all the colts I'd raised, there was a glitter about him. Many had been as good, as straight, as gaited. But he shone with an otherworldliness. Like the light from a going-away-day. This, I told myself, was the horse. The horse I would keep.

I was raising horses then and buying a few too. Selling them to friends after I knew that they were good for the mountains where trails etched the sides of cliffs and predictability was important in an unpredictable land. I wanted to raise good horses for good friends and good homes. There was no profit in it. And this one, I thought, would be the one I would not sell, not even to my best friend.

As he grew, his colt coat darkened and changed and by the time he was a yearling, he was a striking chocolate-brown with flecks of white here and there. I'd seen a grizzly that color once, moving in shadowed timber, turning over rocks and digging roots and easing with a fluidity almost like water over stone. The bear took my breath away and so did the horse. I raised him and I trained him and I was the only person who ever got on his back. In the first years, he was stubborn and my training methods certainly not as refined as the best horseman, but still, we formed a partnership. I got a book on horse training and I learned as he learned and an old horseman neighbor named Bub stopped by and gave advice and praise. The horse grew.

All good horsemen know that there is no "me and my horse" with the truly great horses. It is always "we." A true partnership as if man and horse are one thing, thinking and moving together, watching each other's back. It got to be this way by his third summer when we went into the high Winds to resupply backpackers. We covered many miles. And miles are what define a horse, what make him. There is no substitute for a wet saddle blanket on a young horse. Later that fall after months of packing groceries into the high country, he packed my winter's meat, deer and elk. By the time he had matured, he stood sixteen hands, a honed, muscled, ripped machine of a horse that could walk the horseshoes off of any horse in the country. He never seemed to tire and could walk for days on tough ground. I thought he was nearly perfect in all ways. Even the most particular could find no fault. I was his only partner and he was mine.

That special horse that eases your mind even when you are not riding him. You can look across summer pasture, see him out there grazing, and the troubles of the day fade away. Stress, the burdens of life, the woes of love lost, checkbooks bloodied with red ink, jobs tangled with conflict, living's encumbrances . . . they fall away from just the sight of a good horse out there. Walk out there and touch him, hug him around the neck, and those tribulations are lost to the wind. Ride him and they are gone altogether. That horse had that effect on me.

By the time we ended up in Montana, it seemed we shared the same brain. I have friends who ride good cutting horses and they can relate. The horse knows what you are thinking before you think it. On a cow horse, it is called cow sense. On a mountain horse, it is trail sense.

It was uncanny. I could ride him and think about stepping in a particular direction and, without cue, he would step that direction. Perhaps after a decade of only me as his rider, he knew my heart as I knew his. This continued with the beat of time and hoof: a solo trip into the high country for a week, riding trails where oxygen was thin but elk signs thick, fishing in the evenings, reading a good book in the mornings, and riding on; packing an elk off a snow-choked ridge, busting through heavy drifts that came to the big horse's chest, pounding down to where the elk could be quartered and loaded; riding on a summer evening in a ground-eating lope that was as comfortable as sitting in a padded recliner. Together.

The end came, as most ends do, long before I was ready. It was supposed to be an easy summer weekend in the mountains, back in the Lee Metcalf Wilderness, only six miles in. Fishing. Drinking beer with friends. Laughs. The friends were learning how to horsepack and I told them I would help. At the trailhead, I showed them how to throw camping gear onto pack horses and at camp, I showed them how to disperse their horses in a mountain meadow, hobbling some. We'd picket Grizz, and he'd ground the herd. I pounded the heavy steel picket pin into the ground with a hatchet and tied the length of rope between it and his right front hoof so he could graze in a taut circle. We stoked up a campfire and had our laughs as the sun faded out of the sky. Between the laughs, you could hear the sounds of the horses snorting and munching in lush summer grass, a sound that brings peace to a horseman's soul.

We turned in well after dark, crawling into warm sleeping bags. Late that night a storm came up out of the west, splattering rain against the tent. I snuggled deeper into the bag and listened for the clink of hobble and the snort of a content horse. They were out there, sweet and easy on mountain meadow, despite the storm.

At dawn, in thin light, I heard a sudden commotion as the horses bolted, spooked, ran.

Camp long enough with horses and you learn to sleep light and so when they ran off, I was already pulling on my boots. I didn't think Grizz had pulled his picket, but when I got up, they were all gone. Grizz, like all the horses, had galloped across the meadow, only he was attached by a rope to a swinging piece of sharp steel.

They only ran fifty yards. I walked up to them, a halter in my hand, heading for Grizz, who stood looking at me. In the growing light, I could see his blaze shining.

"What are you doing, you goofy buggers?"

I stepped and the dawn swelled and something was wrong. There was blood running out of one of his nostrils. He took a step toward me.

"You aren't hurt, are you? What happened?"

He took another step toward me, grunted twice, a sound that even today rips at my heart. And he went down. In his right side, back where those big bellows of lung come to a point, was a perfect, round hole. The picket pin. Two-feet-long, sharp. A weapon.

It only took him perhaps ten minutes to die. I screamed and cried and I watched the light fade out of his eyes and off of his coat forever. It happened that quickly, as fast as you can read these sentences and it has stayed with me for years.

It is a humbling thing for a man to walk out of the mountains carrying his saddle over his shoulder and leaving his other self behind.

I wonder, sometimes, about those great cavalrymen and their horses. The depth of pain when that mount went down. The sense of loss as the fire went out. Eleven-thousand mounted French tore across the battlefields of Eylau in 1807 against Russian infantry.

One-and-a-half-million horses died in our Civil War. Our empires were built on the back of equine.

Truly, Heaven has one hell of a horse herd.

FIFTEEN

A Horse for Clare

—

When you were tiny and squalling, I carried you out to the horse pasture and we stood among them and listened. As soon as we were in them, among them, you quieted. Switched off the noise, turned on the attention. As they grazed and we smelled them. There's nothing like the smell of horses.

You would point a tiny finger at each of the horses.

"That one."

I would walk over and place you on an equine back. Hold you there. If the horse walked off, I still had ahold of you and we could move to another horse. No halter, just horses in a pasture, smelling a little girl in my arms and you smelling them back.

Usually the horse did not walk off. It knew.

Old Mac, all of twenty-eight and long retired.

"That one."

Big Red, way up there. Holding on tight, two tiny fists tangled in mane. A massive, powerful horse usually charged with lightening but quiet as an old dairy cow when a child was aboard.

"That one."

Good, gentle, homely Marv.

"That one."

Black Jack, impressive flowing mane, coal-black hide.

We would walk among eight horses and you would be astride every one of them, if only for a moment. The eighth horse, the one that seemed extra special—and always the final one—was June.

She was born on this ranch in the heart of June, a colorful little filly with good breeding and fine long stockings and a big, wide blaze. Trademarks of her line, those markings. Put together well. I named her Calamity June. She is grown now. She will not be very big, but she's as pretty a horse as I have ever raised. "That horse is going to make a little girl really happy some day," a friend said to me once. I thought to myself, "I know just the girl, a little calamity in her own right."

Early on, I had designs for June, thinking, maybe, that she'd be a horse I might ride one day as my new number one. But she did not grow much in that first year, or in that second, or even in that third. By the time I started to work with her in the round pen, she was a nice pony-sized horse. Too small for a man. Just right for a little girl, a little girl who calls me Buddy. Just right for you.

You and I met on a river.

Cold water. Clear. A river of trout and the promise of day.

Your mom went into the hardware store and left me to watch you, a blonde-haired, blue-eyed beauty who was not even two. No problem. But when you projectile-vomited because Mom was gone for fifteen minutes, doubt crept in. I do not get along well with human vomit.

Your mom has the prettiest fly cast in the land and can row a drift boat with flawless precision. She is a fine rider and I taught her to tie a basket hitch in only one showing. But barf before breakfast, before the boat was even on the water? I didn't know.

Then we were with the river and the wailing that would have shamed a suckling pig turned into happy babble. Chatter. A switch had been flipped. The river took us from the boat ramp, over cobble and sand, down riffle. We landed on a midstream island and cast

165

nymphs into a run and you tottered on the bank and collected rocks. I caught one nice rainbow, then put the fly rod in the boat and helped you find heart-shaped rocks. The fishing was forgotten.

We have been aboard that boat many times and it is always the same. Horses too. Walk among them and sit astride them and it is as if you have climbed to a new plane, a new plateau where the loudness of the world is forgotten. Horse and girl live here and it is magical. There is peace here.

I think about the children of this country sometimes, especially when I see them in our cities. Most have their heads down and don't look where they are going. The adults are like this too, pounding the sidewalks, engrossed in texting or yabbering on phones. Earth rotates. Humans mutate.

We go camping. We look at the night sky. You lie between Mom and me in a chaotic nest of blankets and sleeping bags, watching for falling stars. In the morning, we get up and you run around half-naked and cover yourself in dirt, then rinse off in the tiny stream near camp. We look for bugs and squirrels and wildflowers growing in wet edges of meadows. We walk the pines and happy prattle comes with us.

Back in the truck and then back home, plugged-in, carping, and discontent. A pattern emerges.

You were just a toddler when you rode a horse with your Mom for the first time. You both got on Marv and you rode up the ranch road and you waved to the *amera*. All any of us could do was smile. We got you a pink cowboy hat and pink chaps and you were styling. You still wear that hat and those chaps, and you go out to the barn and climb into a saddle in the tack room and pretend that you are roping a cow when you are roping compliant farm dogs.

We spent your third birthday on the river. We cooked a birthday cake in a Dutch oven over coals of fir and alder, listening in the fading day to the river toss and turn on its limestone bed. That day, your favorite present was a skwala stonefly that crawled up your little hand onto your arm and a red heart-shaped rock I found on a gravel bar. Turning three outside. That's the way to celebrate a year gone by and a year coming on.

You're four now and you remember where you were on your third birthday and you can remember that first ride. You talk about skwala presents and heart-shaped rocks and when I am out in the field, walking behind a gun dog, or riding Jack up a ridge that whispers to me of bull elk, I think of you. Sometimes, I'll find a pretty rock and put it into my pocket or my saddlebag and bring it home. On a river this summer, I found the top half of a mussel shell, polished and glittering like an oyster shell from the ocean.

You laughed when you saw it and asked me, "Buddy, an animal lives in there?"

"Yes, honey, that was his home."

This is my first go-around in helping to shape a human life at such an early stage. Maybe I'm not doing it right and maybe I'm making all kinds of mistakes. But when you scrape a knee from falling off a buck-and-rail fence, or get a splitter after playing in the woodpile, or a rash on your butt from sitting bare on a bale of hay, I somehow think of those wounds as cleaner, more honest than those of the city kids. Maybe I'm wrong.

But I think there's a rightness in the way of the soil. I think there's something to be said for a life being jostled by a pack of bird dogs, or nuzzled by a herd of mountain horses, climbed by the barn cats, pecked by hens on the nest. When you bury yourself in black dirt to your little elbows in the garden helping Mom, or construct castles in the sandbox nearby, I know a happy kid when I see one. Inside four walls, you glower. Outside, you glitter. You ask to go horseback riding and fishing and camping. It doesn't matter if the stream is the one that runs through the ranch or the camping is in the horse pasture, or the horseback riding is in the corral. It is outside and you ask. I love that.

So I am working with June and making sure she will be safe for a little girl to ride when you are old enough to ride her on your own. I see a day when our family goes into the mountains for a long week of camping and horseback riding. In that dream, I see you on June, smiling, riding your own horse, crossing rivers and bridges. I see you as a tough Montana girl who has the whole world ahead of her and believes she can do anything because she's mounted on a good horse and she has the trail ahead. There is nothing but trail ahead.

Some day when the world comes up to greet you outside this place, you may not know a salad fork from a dinner fork and the plugged-in world may be a foreign land. But you will know how to throw a double-diamond hitch on a pack horse, find good feed for your herd in the mountains, work the clutch on an old Ford, row a boat, cast a fly line, swing a shotgun. You'll know where to put the crosshairs and when the job is done, you'll know where to start with the knife. You will know a good horse when you see one and you'll have enough common sense to pass on the bad ones. You'll know how to bake a cake in a Dutch oven and clean a mess of brook trout for dinner. And you'll know that there are stars in the sky and you will own a horse named June to ride beneath them.

SIXTEEN

Deep Wild

—

On the last night, the eighth, we found a hole in the mountains. Mountain men would not have called it a hole, for it was only an acre or two. Jackson's Hole—now that was a hole—a vast stretch of flat in a land of up and down. But to me and the ladies, this was meadow enough and a refuge all the same. A tiny pocket meadow among the lodgepoles and aspens, a little glade with hip-high grass, enough to feed three horses. From their direction came the sound of snorting and munching and little else. It had been a long trip. A hundred miles behind us. Twenty-five left.

Three mares and one tired bird dog. I had pulled the packs and the saddles from the mares, fed the dog. Working in the kind of practiced manner that comes with days in the mountains, a routine. The first days are always a bit of a stagger, a stumble. But after a few days, the rhythm comes, the system, everything in its place. Hobbles on the mares, but they hardly needed them, for they were tired and hungry and ready for the stop. One last camp in the mountains. One last day in the wild.

Tomorrow, I would ride up out of the canyon bottom, out of my little pocket of grass into the lodgepole and over the ridge, connecting with a road at the top of the rim, a two-track heading south out of the mountains, into the aspens, beyond. My truck would be there at the trailhead. One hundred twenty-five miles of mountain behind us, nine days. The last six alone, a solo trip to feed some wild thing inside of me that needed to be fed. Even though I do not really understand it. A quest. A need. A challenge. All of those. More.

But now it was sated.

There was an old fire ring. A stream full of cutthroat beyond. I could fish. Thought about it, leaning back against an old log, Sage curled up against my leg. Thought about getting up, leaving the dog, stretching fly line into ferrule, casting and working up the stream. It called to me. But I was tired. Bone-tired. I ached with hard work. A good ache of muscle and sinew moved, worked. But a deep soreness kept me anchored where I was.

I had fished. I had shot a few blue grouse. Mostly, I had ridden. Up some of the toughest trail I'd ever ridden. North to south on the spine of the Wyoming Range. All of it. An entire mountain range with deep timber, high, open slopes, rushing streams, waterfalls, rock fall, scree, and avalanche chutes. And all kinds of weather. Now whatever was behind me on the trail was, at times, little more than a concept on a map. Trail without switchbacks, trail that was no trail at all, trail that was a jumble of dead timber that I had to pick my way through for days. Once, the trail disappeared into fog and my heart rose in my chest as I lost it, uncertain above timberline if I was riding toward a cliff edge or toward the way out. My intended route had changed and re-changed as the terrain, the weather, and the trails dictated direction. I had told friends where I would be, but if they went looking, I'd be somewhere else. Such moves are never wise. Route changes in the middle of the trip are rookie moves. But I had had little choice.

A hundred miles ago, I parked the truck, left the keys where my shuttle driver could find them. Loaded a pack horse, saddled two ride horses, met a friend who would join me for the first three days of my trip. Traveling light. Before us was an adventure, an ascending trail, trout streams to cross, ridges to ride. A fly rod behind the saddle. A shotgun in the scabbard. Hunt and fish and ride down the backbone of Wyoming's least-known mountain range. Most of the route was on a so-called national recreation trail that turned out to be a dim path in tough country. While we were out, it would change from late summer to autumn and the calendar would shift from August and into September. On the first day of that great short month that starts the season of the hunt, I would swing my shotgun on mountain grouse, I hoped. Until then, we would ride and fish.

Now, with a tiny fire at my feet and a good setter curled up on my thigh, I had nothing left in the tank. I was exhausted. Tired. The quest for adventure, the feeding of that wild inside was done. Days earlier, I had the drive to throw saddles and loads. This evening, fire popping, a last sip of the last night's bourbon in the flask, I had nothing. So I sat and listened to the stream, to horses snort and munch, to chickadees chattering in the spruce. I rewarmed the stir-fry blue grouse I'd made the night before. Tried to share it with the dog, but she was too tired to eat. She was thin now, and footsore. I could feel hard muscle through her hide. My own hide was tighter too, summer fat gone in a week's worth of hard work. And so I rested and I thought about what was behind me.

An unknown trail now known. Steeper than I had imagined, tougher. Slick in rain, covered by deadfall in some places. Disappearing into the tundra in others. I had worn out the topo maps I carried in the pocket of my chaps, pulling them out again and again to make sure I was on course. Lightening had chased me out of the high country. My known route had been altered to an unknown one. Mistakes, if I made them, had consequences that grew increasingly grave with each hoofprint. It poured rain. Snowed. I tucked myself into a thick coat, glad for good gloves, batwing chaps, long underwear, a riding slicker. I'd seen less than ten people the whole time I'd been out and those only near the road I had left miles behind.

Once, a day or so after my riding companion had left on day three, I came across a thick green whitebark pine lying across the trail. A tree that blocked the trail completely. Without cutting it, there was no way through. The trail fell away steeply, too steep to ride around. Dull panic rose, then was swallowed behind tight jaw. I had no choice.

It took me two hours to cut through the pine with a handsaw. It took everything I had to push the heavy log off the trail, even with the help of gravity. The horses, tired, heads down, were back a quarter mile in the timber, waiting. We rode on as evening fell, making for a camp before dark.

In another place, I came to a tangle of deadfall on a steep slick side hill in the pouring rain. When I dismounted to move a log from the trail, I slipped on the gumbo and slid on my backside right under my saddle horse. She just stood there. I was covered in mud, lost my hat, trembling in the cold rain. Somehow I managed to get back aboard.

There was no turning back. My truck was ahead, not behind. There was no out other than forward. I pressed on.

One morning, I lost the trail for an hour in thick fog, working well above timberline, riding from rock cairn to rock cairn and waiting for the wind to shift the fog for the next move. Once, I snaked all three horses down a switchback that was too steep to ride, praying they wouldn't slip and fall onto me. When I looked back up at the last horse, it seemed as if she were floating in the air twenty feet over my head. It felt that vertical.

And so it went. Snow one morning. Sage pointing blue grouse on a ridge top and the shots rattling and echoing off the cliffs. Dropping two birds for dinner, breakfast, and lunch. And dinner again. Could have killed a dozen in my days on the mountain, but one can only eat and carry so many. And now, the last night and the fire popping. From the timber, far above my little glen, I hear an elk bugle and across the canyon, an answer.

Wild country. Wilderness. Bad consequences for poor decisions. Challenge met. A foot-sore bird dog and tired horses. Nothing but the talk of chickadees and bull elk and the roll of a trout stream going by. And a deep fatigue that bolts me to the forest floor. I will sleep deeply tonight, lulled by starlight, listening to elk on the mountain, horses in the meadow, stream at my side, and the warmth of a good, tired bird dog on my flank.

I wouldn't have it any other way.

SEVENTEEN

What's Left of Lefty

—

Two years ago on a snapping-cold, very late November day, I woke to the sound of one of my horses whinnying.

Horses whinny. But if you live on the same ground as a herd of horses, you know they rarely do so when everything is right with the equine world. They neigh because they miss their buddies. So in that cold light and bitter wind, I went to see what was the trouble.

There he stood, the little bay gelding I called Lefty. He was a people horse, the kind that you had to shoo away when you were walking in the pasture. The kind that you just flat-out liked. That made you smile. I had designs for him that coming spring, plans to make him my new number one. Those plans were not to be realized.

He stood at the edge of the south pasture, his butt to the shelter provided by a nearby building. The other horses were a quarter mile away. And Lefty didn't like it. He was calling for them, but not moving toward them. Immediately, in that gut-raw knowing that is part of being a horseman, I knew something was very wrong.

A bone, broken and ragged, stuck out from his leg below the right knee.

It is one of the great ironies of the world that something so strong and so powerful and wonderful as a horse is so delicate. The heart of a warrior is propped up by pencil legs. The might that has carried man into battle, built his cities, plowed his crops, run down his meat on the hoof, is carried by stilts of straw. Legs and horses. No horse survives a broken leg. A compound fracture especially.

There was no calling a vet. There was nothing to do. Check that. There was only one thing to do. I walked to my gun cabinet and loaded a pistol.

It is a humbling, sickening, horrible task to put down an animal you love on your own. Having a veterinarian do it is one thing. Pulling the trigger yourself is another.

For a long time on that last day of November, I sat and talked to Lefty's cooling body. He had been special, a funny pal. I knew that there would be no burying or any landfill for him. It would not be right. Instead, I would drag Lefty to the upper pasture, over the thin snow to the back fence.

I had been seeing eagles on the roads for a few weeks. Big, stunning golden and bald eagles. Perched on fence posts. Sometimes slow in flight from a road-killed deer on the centerline. I slowed down, watched them lumber off, bellies full, climbing with that flapping, huge span of wing.

For a couple weeks after Lefty's last day, I didn't walk up there. He lay in the open, between clumps of sage and bunch grass. A beautiful little bay horse no more.

Then one day in December just before Christmas, I decided to pay him a visit. New snow had fallen a few days before and as I walked up there on that sagebrush-clad bench, enjoying the tingling-crisp winter day, I began to pick up tracks. Small tracks, not much longer than an inch from toe to heel. I kneeled in the snow. Fox, I guessed. I rose, brushed snow from my jeans, walked on. Still not near Lefty's carcass, still several hundred yards away. Picked up larger canine tracks. Kneeled again. Measured. Coyote. I looked ahead and saw an eagle, a huge bald eagle, on the jack-leg fence near where Lefty lay two hundred yards to the north. The eagle took off clumsily as I approached. I followed a sharply-defined path of fox and coyote tracks. A trail. I even found the tracks of what I surmised was an insomniac skunk out of hibernation for a mid-winter adventure. I prepared myself as I came closer to where I'd left Lefty two weeks before. And I looked.

Lefty was gone. In his place was a skeleton, mane and tail hair and stomach contents, just a bit of hide, some reddish scraps bright in the white canvas of new snow. That was it. Around the carcass were dozens, hundreds of tracks. Eagle tracks blended in with coyote and fox and skunk tracks. Lots of eagle tracks. I watched the eagle I had flushed from the fence peel toward the western skyline, then turn to a leaf-bare cottonwood down by the creek.

For two more weeks, the eagles came to the ranch. They perched in pairs and threes and fours in the cottonwoods and when they flew off to the north, toward the bench, I knew where they were going.

It almost felt as if Lefty was flying with them.

EIGHTEEN

Last Ride

—

In the evenings, when the rest of us are in camp, he stands out there in the meadow. He looks off at the mountain once in a while, but usually, he stands next to his old game warden horse and rests a hand on its strong withers while the old bay grazes and hops in hobbles to the next clump of grass. I have watched him do this for the last several nights while we have worked around camp, chopping wood, laughing, the sounds and smells of dinner coming from the wall tent. Sometimes he cradles a mug with a good slug of

Kentucky bourbon in the other hand and he sips and touches the old horse. Once, I started out there to visit, but turned back. I did not belong out there.

We are about a half-dozen miles back there, a comfortable camp with good grass for the horses, good shade for the meat pole, good times for the hunters. Elk have been talking on the mountain and on the first morning before light, a herd filtered right through the meadow. We could hear them, but we could not see them.

I do not see the old horse often these days, just once or twice a year, but that is enough. Seeing him makes me realize he is getting older, for each time I do, it seems as if his withers are a bit steeper, his back a bit more swayed, a few more wrinkles and creases at the corner of his mouth, more gray around the eyes. I wonder if my friend sees this too, or if the familiarity of seeing your horse every day is enough varnish to cover the obvious. For me, it is like going to your high school reunion, seeing an old friend, and thinking, "Wow, he's gained some weight. And lost some hair." Daily contact might gloss such changes.

But I think my friend knows that there are not many more trails ahead of Todd. The fast bay is slower and his neck doesn't arch into the reins as it once did. He no longer thinks there's a mare over every ridge. These are things that are obvious and that cannot be coated over with the familiarity. He knows. I can read it on him, a sadness. I can see it in his shoulders, the tilt of his head. The horse used to square them up and put a swell of pride there. Now it is as if he carries the weight of it all.

He is out there now, hand on Todd's back, the gold light of September splashing across the man and the horse and the mountain meadow. The horse snorts in the tall grass and then dinner is ready. He walks to the wall tent with his head down.

In the morning, we split. Three of us one way. Jim and Dave another. Our trio works up the long ridge that leads to the top of Wildcat, hiking hard and looking for an elk sign. We don't see much until we reach the green timber on the peak's back flank. There, in the cool, wet grass where a small spring seeps out of the mountain, we find a wallow and we slow down, walking softly and feeling elk nearby. We climb the mountain, smelling and watching for elk and then in the distance, we hear shots. One. Then another.

The shots come from the burn, the place where Jim and Dave went this morning. We work to another ridge, where we can peer down into the burnt timber, a huge patch of country where the fires burned hot and fast, taking everything. In the first year or two after, the burn was empty and dead, void of elk and life. But now the grass grows hip-deep and the elk feel safe there. Dead trees are littered across the ground, thrown by the wind like a game of pick-up-sticks. Some hunters will not go in there because of the deadfall, but the elk are there.

The day washes away while we wonder about the shots. This is one of the great joys of hunting, not knowing if others in your party have seen or taken game, the stories yet to be told. In the afternoon, we work back down the ridge, skirting the burn where Jim and Dave disappeared in the morning.

"Hey!"

Dave pops up over the ridge, carrying a pack that looks heavy. Then Jim comes up the ridge, packing his rifle, looking tired. We stop, wondering, ready for the story.

My friend has been hunting for six decades and has taken many bull elk. But the one he took this morning is the bull of his life. Dave is packing its cape, a heavy load from a big herd bull. The story comes.

They heard the bull and his rivals talking in the burn, and eased to the edge of a little canyon. Dave was carrying a muzzle-loader and when they peered down into the hole where the herd grazed, he knew he was too far away for a good shot. It was up to Jim.

He took his time. He placed his hat on a log and snuggled up against the skin of it and when the big herd bull stepped into view that was all there was. The bull died with his rack arched gracefully up over a log and the two hunters walked to the edge of the canyon and looked off into the burn. The canyon was steep even for a man, too steep for a horse. They scrambled down and then into the burn and started the hard work. Jim knew he would probably never shoot another bull such as this one and he told Dave to go hunting while he worked on the cape.

By afternoon, Dave circled back and found Jim dozing in the September sunlight, the big elk quartered and ready to go out. By the time they worked up out of the burn and found us on the trail, the light had faded from the day and camp was still several miles away. Tomorrow, we will begin the long pack out.

Snuggled into the wall tent, we talk logistics. Leaving an elk out overnight in grizzly country is never a good idea, but sometimes, there are no other options. The three of us decide to ride for the big bull in the morning, taking two pack horses. It is tough country for men and horses, a mountain of burned and downed trees to skirt, miles of bogs and wet meadows. I pull out a map and look at it hard, spread it out on the ground inside the wall tent. We crouch around it and trace a finger over a possible route down to the elk.

At first light, we mount three good horses and lead two others. Jim and Todd, me on the black stallion, Ace, and Randy on Lad. Jim leads out. Up. In the grayness, we ride silently, working up the old trail, easing around deadfall, stepping the horses over logs when we can. There is only the sound of horse hooves on mountain trail and the occasional snort. We do not talk until we hit the base of the mountain where a steep slope rises in the final pitch to the summit. Last night, we thought this would be the place to go around the mountain. We cannot go straight to the elk because of the small canyon. We have to go up and around and then come in from above. In the generic sameness of the burn, it may be tough to find the bull, but we have all day.

It is hard going, for at the base of the mountain there are cut ravines that we must ride down and then up. Some are twenty, even thirty feet deep. The horses step gracefully, though, and then we are in the burn and we zigzag between deadfalls, the black-charred limbs scraping our shirtsleeves, the horses working harder now and the smell of their sweat mingling with the scent of the mountain. The sun is up hard and hot and a trickle of sweat trails down my back. More of it beads up under my hat. Todd works the lead, carefully, slowly, and we drop down through the burn.

We work back and forth in it, stepping over old logs and then Jim pulls up.

"I have to admit it, I think I'm confused. Why don't we tie up the horses here, and I'll work down through the burn. I'll fire off a pistol shot if I find it."

It sounds like a pretty good plan and we step off our horses. Everywhere there are burnt trees, but there is good grass too. The slope is steep, but the horses can move there and graze, and maybe we can find the elk yet.

We doze in the tall grass and listen to the horses graze, their lead ropes trailing out between their hooves. The ride has been hard work for them and they are hungry. They aren't going anywhere.

An hour later, we hear the crack of a pistol shot down below us, then another and we rise and gather horses. We string them out behind us and work down through the timber, zigging west, then zagging east and then stopping. Another pistol shot cracks the air and we work toward the sound and come to the edge of a small ridge. There, below us, amid the burnt timber and elk wallow, is Jim. We step the horses over logs and come up on him.

It takes us a long time to heft the big bull onto the pack horses. The hindquarters in particular are massive and it is all Randy and I can do to lift one at a time while Jim holds the top of the sawbuck so the saddle will not turn on the horse.

I tie a double diamond, then we load the front quarters, which are massive in their own right, and place the huge rack, seven points to a side, over them and I throw another double diamond.

Jim takes one last look around. The sunlight is filtering through the burn, casting long shadows like the bars of a jail cell over everything. The canyon rim where Jim lay to shoot in the only patch of green timber anywhere around is above us and east. Below and above and behind there is nothing but burn. The place reeks of elk, and the wallows are muddy, and the ground is torn.

"He had his herd in a pretty good place, didn't he?"

There's a sadness in my friend's voice and he turns to his old bay horse, left hand up on the saddle horn, turning the stirrup and swinging up in one fluid motion, one easy movement. I've always admired how he makes it look so easy. He leads off through the burnt timber, up and back the way we came in, riding his old bay horse, leading the pack horse laden with the antlers from the bull of his lifetime.

Perhaps it is my imagination, but there seems to be a bit of an arch in Todd's neck and my friend's shoulders are squared up. He's looking off ahead, up the mountain.

NINETEEN

Trailheads and Trailends

—

In the sweet calm warmth of an early fall day, you come to a meadow, a big one. It stretches east and west, an island of grass in a sea of timber. This is far-back country, so far back that you feel as if you are descending years instead of ascending a trail. At the trailhead, a sign talked of things wild—of grizzlies and campfires and wilderness. This, you realize, is what it's all about, about wild. Wildlife and wilderness and a good mountain horse. Those words belong in the same sentence and that sentence is your hunt.

191

You have been in this place before and never before. This year, the trail is new, but the sense of bigness, of wild, is the same. Last year, it was the Fitzpatrick Wilderness. This year, it is the Teton. Next year, perhaps it will be the same, or perhaps it will be another. But you know that without wilderness, your hunt would be very different. It would have a different texture and a different feel. This is the place you go when the words you say about the last place are "there's gettin' to be too many hunters here."

At the meadow, you work quickly to unload heavily laden pack horses, moving with the ease of the years, cooing softly to good mountain horses, touching soft noses, whispering a light hand down a sweaty neck. You work rope and pannier and you dig down for the hobbles and the picket. You find a place out there in that island where the mare can work grass on her picket. Enough to keep fit for a week's hunt. The rest of the herd goes into the meadow too, some with hobbles and some nothing at all. Another mare, with a soul as tame as an old dog, walks about the meadow freer that she does in pasture back home. She has always been like this, ever since you brought her back from Missouri as a two-year-old filly. Now the mare is old and still sweet. Up here, in this high place of wapiti and grizzly, she could walk all the way back down the trail to the old pickup, or she could point her blue roan nose north and be in Montana in a week or so without crossing one fence. That is the definition of freedom, but she will stay because her friends are here and so is the grass. A young mule gets the same treatment. Mules love mares. Two picketed mares will hold an army of mules.

After the horses are cared for, camp goes together quickly. There's a wall tent for cooking and, away and upwind, there are two tents for sleeping. It is grizz country and you walk with respect and caution. You sleep away from grizzly food because you do not want to become grizzly food. The panniers stay at the cook tent, and everything else goes up on a pole, out of bear reach. It is work, but this kind of work has a reward and that reward is wild country and wildlife.

Before dawn, you rise and walk to the cook tent between small lodgepoles through the last tall grass of summer. The stars are brilliant, brighter than you remembered them from last year. It is dark, so dark. Sometimes, in other places, you can see the far-off shine of city lights in a night sky, but up here, there is nothing. You could be at the end of the earth, or the beginning. You see the Big Dipper, and, more importantly, Orion the Hunter, his belt and his sword. It will be a good day today.

After breakfast and in the dim light of predawn, you work up through the pines and spruce, following a thin trail made by elk, working higher. You walk into an old burn and start to pick up elk tracks. You surmise that the elk are shading up in green timber, then working the burn at night. If you are right, you will pick up more tracks at the edge of the timber, still in the burn, but near cover. The timber gives shelter, the burn provides food. All day you work up through a mosaic of timber and burn, walking softly and carrying a good bow. The elk are here, but not close enough. You see lots of them, big bulls, smaller ones, ever-watchful cows, calves.

The next day follows a similar pattern, a system that your being swings into as easily as you swing aboard that good walking-out gelding that you ride. Rise, check the stock, eat, walk, listen, smell, eat, look, feel, walk, check the stock, eat, sleep. And over again. One day you see a pine marten deep in the timber and he watches you, curious. Perhaps this is the first human he has ever seen. Another day, you watch a big grizzly, a four-hundred-pounder, work across an open slope five hundred yards away, dining on currants and elderberries, working into the breeze, his golden hide rippling like grass before a prairie wind. Once, deep in the woods, you see an animal that is black and catlike and think that perhaps you have seen a fisher, a rare sight. You hear a wolf one morning. You jump two big bull moose from a patch of green timber in the old burn on another. Deer bound from day beds every morning and you are into elk every day. What a game country.

At night, you jot these things down in a journal you have kept of every hunt before and you vow to keep these things going, for when you are old and toothless and blinded by years, perhaps you can convince someone to read from this journal, to stimulate that old brain and send it back to a wild place.

But now, there is a mountain to climb and a wild place to hunt. This wild place, this wilderness, speaks of another time and of this time. And you think how fortunate you are to live in an age where you can still feel the true wild, the last of it.

When you do finally get close enough to an elk to bring an arrow to its mark, you bend to that warm body and you ply a sharp knife, sweating from the work. And as you leave the place where the elk fell, you stop and turn and you make this wish: may there always be a place to hunt, where Orion shows clear in the hour before predawn, where the lights of no city invade, where elk browse in the goodness of a long-ago fire, where freedom means a place wild enough that an old blue mare can walk clean to Montana without hitting barbwire. If she wants to.

$$\cup$$

On a warm spring day, Jim led Todd out into a horse pasture in the shadow of the Tobacco Root Mountains, up in Montana. The sounds and smells of new fresh life arriving on the land were all around and the Jefferson River was thick with meltwater, but Todd was drawn down hard by winter and done. The trails of Wyoming and Colorado were off south and years behind and now there was only a Montana spring morning and an old horse on his last walk. The bay followed his partner easily on a slack rope into a place where a backhoe had done fresh work. The veterinarian stepped toward the old horse's head while Jim fed him a pan of oats and thought about those trails and those rides. Todd's head sagged.

There are no more mountains for the mountain mare. Her friend Bob did not make it through the winter. His good heart gave out after seventy-some years. I hope one of his last thoughts was of riding the mountain lady into the Wyoming high country and that wherever he is, he is well-mounted and the horse is plumb gentle.

The pain of that loss was on all of us months later when the good bay mare broke a hind leg in the pasture. We didn't know how it happened and it felt as if the world was swallowing us up with the loss when I thought about Bob and that mountain lady and how they were both gone now. I told Dave that maybe Bob needed a good horse to ride wherever he was. Somehow, it helped.

She is a very old lady now and has gone completely white. But that is really her only sign of age. White. There is no sway to her back, no lack of fire in her heart. She is pushing thirty years old, this Machine, and she still can walk as good as anything in the country. But there are younger horses with hills to climb and she has earned her retirement in a pasture of belly-deep grass. When the time comes, she will not leave this place with its cottonwoods along a laughing little trout stream and its wide bench of sagebrush where the eagles soar in the winter and the meadowlarks call for the commencement of spring.

Bill is still riding toward Canada.